AMAZING ASTRAL PROJECTION

How To Astral Travel, Have Complete Lucid Control Over Your Celestial Body And Powerful Journeys Through Dreaming and Astroprojection

Melissa Gomes

>> https://smartpa.ge/MelissaGomes<<

© Copyright 2022 by Melissa Gomes

All Rights Reserved.

No part of this publication may be reproduced, distributed, or transmitted in any form or by any means, including photocopying, recording, or other electronic or mechanical methods, without the prior written permission of the publisher, except in the case of brief quotations embodied in reviews and certain other noncommercial uses permitted by copyright law.
Disclaimer: This book provides accurate and authoritative information regarding the subject matter. By its sale, neither the publisher nor the author is engaged in rendering psychological or other professional services. If expert assistance or counseling is needed, the services of a competent professional should be sought.

Table of Contents

- **TABLE OF CONTENTS** 3
  - BONUS 1: FREE WORKBOOK - VALUE 12.95$ 7
  - BONUS 2: FREE BOOK - VALUE 12.95$ 8
  - BONUS 3: FREE AUDIOBOOK - VALUE 14.95$ ..... **Error! Bookmark not defined.**
  - JOIN MY REVIEW TEAM! .... **Error! Bookmark not defined.**
  - FOR ALL THE FREEBIES, VISIT THE FOLLOWING LINK: **Error! Bookmark not defined.**
- **I'M HERE BECAUSE OF YOU** .... ERROR! BOOKMARK NOT DEFINED.
- **CHAPTER 1: INTRODUCTION TO ASTRAL PROJECTION** 8
  - WHAT IS ASTRAL PROJECTION? 11
  - DIFFERENT TYPES OF ASTRAL PROJECTION 12
  - DIFFERENT LEVELS OF ASTRAL PROJECTION 14
  - THE HISTORY OF ASTRAL PROJECTION 16
  - ASTRAL PROJECTION AND LUCIDITY 17
- **CHAPTER 2: THE BENEFITS OF ASTRAL PROJECTION** 20
  - OVERCOMING FEAR 20
  - IMPROVED SLEEP QUALITY 21
  - STRESS RELIEF 22
  - INCREASED CREATIVITY 23
  - FASTER LEARNING 25
  - IMPROVED PHYSICAL HEALTH 26
  - EXPLORATION OF NEW WORLDS 27
  - HEAL FROM TRAUMA 29
  - HEAL FROM GRIEF 30
- **CHAPTER 3: PREPARING FOR YOUR FIRST ASTRAL PROJECTION EXPERIENCE** 33
  - CREATING THE RIGHT ENVIRONMENT: 34
  - THE POWER OF BELIEF 35
  - RELAXATION TECHNIQUES 36
  - CLEARING YOUR MIND 37
  - RETRIEVING INFORMATION FROM THE ASTRAL REALM 38
  - RETURNING HOME SAFELY 38
  - DEALING WITH SETBACKS 39
  - CONCLUSION 39

CHAPTER 4: MAIN STEPS OF ASTRAL PROJECTION 41
- THE BODY FALLS ASLEEP 41
- THE CONSCIOUS MIND IS AWARE, BUT THE BODY IS ASLEEP 42
- THE CONSCIOUS MIND AND BODY ARE BOTH AWAKE 42
- TRANSITIONING INTO THE ASTRAL REALM 43
- MOVING AROUND THE ASTRAL REALM 43
- COMMUNICATION IN THE ASTRAL REALM 44
- RETURNING TO YOUR PHYSICAL BODY 44
- TIPS FOR SUCCESSFUL ASTRAL PROJECTION 45
- PITFALLS TO AVOID DURING ASTRAL PROJECTION 45
- FREQUENTLY ASKED QUESTIONS ABOUT ASTRAL PROJECTION 46

CHAPTER 5: YOUR FIRST TIME IN THE ASTRAL REALM 48
- WHAT TO EXPECT 48
- HOW TO NAVIGATE THE ASTRAL REALM 49
- THE CONSCIOUS MIND AND BODY ARE BOTH AWAKE. 50
- TRANSITIONING INTO THE ASTRAL REALM 51
- SEARCHING FOR YOUR HIGHER SELF 52
- MEETING YOUR ANIMAL GUIDES 53
- DISCOVERING YOUR LIFE PURPOSE 53
- EXPLORING YOUR PAST LIVES 54
- RETURN TO YOUR BODY 55

CHAPTER 6: OVERCOMING OBSTACLES TO ASTRAL PROJECTING 56
- FEAR 56
- DOUBT 58
- DISTRACTIONS 59
- INTENSE EMOTIONS 61

CHAPTER 7: THE DIFFERENT TYPES OF ASTRAL PROJECTION 64
- LUCID DREAMS 64
- OUT-OF-BODY EXPERIENCES 66
- REMOTE VIEWING 67
- NEAR-DEATH EXPERIENCES 69
- AFTER-DEATH COMMUNICATIONS 71

CHAPTER 8: BASIC ASTRAL PROJECTION TECHNIQUES 74
- THE ROPE TECHNIQUE 74
- DISPLACED AWARENESS 76
- THE MONROE TECHNIQUE 78
- THE MIRROR TECHNIQUE 80
- THE REM TECHNIQUE 82

    WATCHING YOURSELF SLEEP 84

CHAPTER 9: ADVANCED ASTRAL PROJECTION TECHNIQUES 87

    HYPNOSIS 87
    FOCUS TECHNIQUES 90
    GUIDED VISUALIZATIONS 93
    BREATHWORK 96
    MEDITATION 99
    RETROCOGNITION TECHNIQUE 105
    THE EIDETIC IMAGERY TECHNIQUE 109
    THE RECOLLECTION TECHNIQUE 111

CHAPTER 10: 59 POSITIVE AFFIRMATIONS FOR ASTRAL PROJECTION 114

    59 AFFIRMATIONS FOR ASTRAL PROJECTION 114

FREEBIES! .... ERROR! BOOKMARK NOT DEFINED.

    BONUS 1: FREE WORKBOOK - VALUE 12.95$ ..... **ERROR! BOOKMARK NOT DEFINED.**
    BONUS 2: FREE BOOK - VALUE 12.95$ .... **ERROR! BOOKMARK NOT DEFINED.**
    BONUS 3: FREE AUDIOBOOK - VALUE 14.95$ ..... **ERROR! BOOKMARK NOT DEFINED.**
    JOIN MY REVIEW TEAM! .... **ERROR! BOOKMARK NOT DEFINED.**
    FOR ALL THE FREEBIES, VISIT THE FOLLOWING LINK:**ERROR! BOOKMARK NOT DEFINED.**

I'M HERE BECAUSE OF YOU .... ERROR! BOOKMARK NOT DEFINED.

FREEBIES

AND

RELATED PRODUCTS

**WORKBOOKS
AUDIOBOOKS
FREE BOOKS
REVIEW COPIES**

HERE

HTTPS://SMARTPA.GE/MELISSAGOMES

Freebies!

I have a **special treat for you**! You can access exclusive bonuses I created specifically for my readers at the following link! The link will redirect you to a webpage containing all my books and bonuses for each book. Just select the book you have purchased and check the bonuses!

>> https://smartpa.ge/MelissaGomes<<

OR scan the QR Code with your phone's camera

Bonus 1: Free Workbook - Value 12.95$

This **workbook** will guide you with **specific questions** and give you all the space you need to write down the answers. Taking time for **self-reflection** is extremely valuable, especially when looking to develop new skills and **learn** new concepts. I highly suggest you *grab this complimentary workbook for yourself*, as it will help you gain clarity on your goals. Some authors like to sell the workbook, but I think giving it away for free is the perfect way to say **"thank you" to my readers**.

Bonus 2: Free Book - Value 12.95$

Grab a **free short book** with **22+ Techniques for Meditation**. The book will introduce you to a range of meditation practices you can use to help you develop your inner awareness, inner calm, and overall sense of well-being. You will also learn how to begin a meditation practice that works for you regardless of your schedule. These meditation techniques work for everyone, regardless of age or fitness level. Check it out at the link below!

Bonus 3: Free audiobook - Value 14.95$

If you love listening to audiobooks on the go or would enjoy a narration as you read along, I have great news for you. You can download the audiobook version of ***my books*** for **FREE** just by signing up for a FREE 30-day trial! You can find the audio versions of my books (depending on availability) at the following link.

Join my Review Team!

Are you an avid reader looking to have more insights into spirituality? Do you want to get free books in exchange for an honest review? You can do so by joining my Review Team! You will get priority access to my books before they are released. You only need to follow me on Booksprout, and you will get notified every time a new Review Copy is available for my latest release!

For all the Freebies, visit the following link:

>> https://smartpa.ge/MelissaGomes<<

OR scan the QR Code with your phone's camera.

I'm here because of you

When you're supporting an independent author,
you're supporting a dream. Please leave
an honest review by scanning
the QR code below and clicking on the "Leave a Review" Button.

https://smartpa.ge/MelissaGomes

Chapter 1: Introduction to Astral Projection

What is Astral Projection?

Astral projection is an experience that typically happens during sleep, although it can also happen while awake. It involves the conscious separation of the astral body from the physical body. The astral body is often referred to as the soul or spirit. This experience can be very blissful, and many report feeling a sense of peace and joy.
Others may have more intense experiences, such as flying or moving through walls. There are different types of astral projection experiences, but they all involve the same basic process: you consciously leave your physical body and explore the world in your astral form. Depending on your level of awareness during the experience, you may simply float around aimlessly or be able to direct your movements and explore specific places.
Many people who have had anastatic projections believe that this experience has a spiritual component; they believe that we all have an immortal soul that leaves our physical bodies when we die and goes on to another realm. People who have been through a near-death experience often report having an out-of-body experience at some point during the experience. While it is possible to project your consciousness outside of your body without dying, it's usually accompanied by extreme pain or fear, and it usually stops you from coming out of your physical body again.
Some view this phenomenon from a scientific perspective; they suggest that what we perceive as reality is just electrical signals processed by our brains. Regardless of which camp you fall into,

there's no denying that Astral projection is a fascinating topic worthy of further exploration.

Different types of Astral Projection

There are many different types of astral projection, each resulting in a unique experience. The three most commonly reported types of astral projection are: unconscious, conscious, and lucid. The unconscious type would be the most common type of astral projection. People are asleep when they are projected, and they do not control whether or not they will project.

They have little to no memory of anything that occurred after the projected moment. Occasionally people can recall some memories, but these are usually vague and incoherent. People who have had this type of projection often report certain feelings and sensations just before the projection but no memory of any events immediately after.

Lucid Astral Projection is when a person is aware of what they are doing when they project. It is possible to consciously project while in a state of sleep or consciousness. People who have had this type of projection usually report that they experienced the waking world while consciously projecting. They often report feeling as though they are awake but in their astral body with their body asleep and out of focus. The sensations and feelings associated with this type of projection tend to differ from those associated with unconscious or conscious astral travel, but they often overlap to a certain extent.

Unconscious Astral Projection

Unconscious astral projection occurs when the individual is unaware that they are leaving their body. This type of projection is often associated with sleep paralysis, which can cause individuals to feel as though they are unable to move or speak. Although this can be a frightening experience, it is important to remember that you are safe and will return to your body eventually.

There are two main theories about why people have unconscious astral projections:

1) It is our natural way of dealing with stressful situations.
2) It occurs when we die temporarily, and our soul leaves our body while we enter the afterlife briefly before returning to our physical form again.

Regardless of the reason, individuals who have experienced an unconscious projection report feeling a sense of peace and well-being during the event itself.

Conscious Astral Projection

Conscious astral projection happens when an individual consciously decides to leave their physical body and travel in the astral realm. This can be done through various methods, such as visualization exercises or using specific breathing techniques. People who have completed a conscious projection often report feeling a sense of euphoria and joyousness during the experience. In addition, they also tend to remember their travels quite clearly afterward and can recount them in great detail.

Lucid Astral Projection

Lucid astral projection is similar to conscious projection, except that people become aware that they are dreaming while still in the dream state. This allows them to take control of their environment and explore it freely without worrying about waking up from the dream. Lucid projections are often considered to be some of the most powerful and enlightening experiences, as they offer complete freedom to explore the inner and outer worlds without any limitations.

Although each type of astral projection has benefits, it is not uncommon to experience all three types of projections in a single night. Many people who have had an astral experience report that it can take several weeks or months to fully integrate what they experienced into their current life.

Different levels of Astral Projection

There are different levels of astral Projection, from beginner to advanced. This section will explore the different levels of astral experience and what each entail.

When you begin astral practice, you probably have no prior conscious experience in "astral" travel. In your conscious awareness, you have no direct knowledge, experience, or recollection of ever being in another place or time. Your reality is your physical body and your mind and unconscious mind combined. Your beliefs are that of the physical universe and are mostly realistic and based on facts. As you progress in your Astral practice, you may experience your conscious awareness during the dream state at night or meditation or hypnagogic states during the day. During this stage, you begin to gain your first experiences of what the real world feels like. You begin to

have visions and experiences of other places and times. The dream is a good place to start for this exercise, but feel free to experiment with hypnagogic states.
There are three main levels of astral Projection: **conscious, semi-conscious, and unconscious.**

The first level, **conscious Projection**, is when you are aware that you are projecting your consciousness out of your body and into another realm. You have complete control over your actions in this state and can choose to return to your body at any time.
Semi-conscious Projection occurs when you are not completely aware that you are projecting but may become aware during the experience. You may lose control over your actions in this state and find it difficult to return to your body if you do not know how to use Astral Project correctly.

Unconscious Projection is when you are unaware that you are projecting. This is the most dangerous projection level, as you can get lost in the astral plane and may not be able to find your way back to your body.

Different techniques can be used to achieve each level of Projection. For conscious Projection, it is said that visualization and meditation are the best methods. With semi-conscious Projection, sleep paralysis can be induced to achieve a state where one is between wakefulness and sleep.
It should also be noted that there are different planes of existence within the astral realm, and each experience level corresponds with a different plane. The first level generally takes place on the lower planes closest to our physical world. As we move up through the levels, we begin accessing higher planes which can take us further away from our physical bodies. It is important to note that there is no time limit in which you must reach these levels of experience. Some might reach them

quickly, and others may need years of practice to achieve them. It is a matter of individual experience.

Astral Projection is an ability that we all have. It is projecting one's consciousness out of their physical body and into another realm.

The History of Astral Projection

Astral Projection is a topic that has been debated by many throughout history. Some people believe it is possible to leave your body and travel to other realms, while others believe that it is nothing more than a figment of the imagination. In this section, we will look at some of the historical accounts of astral Projection to see what various cultures and belief systems have had to say about this phenomenon.

The history of astral Projection can be traced back thousands of years to various cultures worldwide. In many cases, those who claimed to have experienced astral Projection were considered Shamans or spiritual leaders in their communities. For example, in ancient China, there was a belief that certain Taoist monks could separate their souls from their bodies and travel great distances. This ability was thought to be attained through meditation and other spiritual practices. Astral Projection also appears in Hindu texts dating back hundreds of years ago. The Vedas, sacred Hindu texts, describe a state called "Swapna," which translates to "dreaming." It is said that during Swapna, one's soul can leave the body and explore different planes of existence. There are also references to astral Projection in ancient Egyptian texts and Native American stories and mythology. These narratives often describe individuals leaving their physical bodies behind to communicate with the spirit world.

While there are many historical accounts of astral Projection, it is important to note that not all can be verified. In some cases, we only have the words of those who claim to have experienced Astral Projection. This makes it difficult to determine whether these individuals were telling the truth about their experiences. Additionally, even if somebody did experience astral Projection, there is no guarantee that they would be able to accurately describe what happened during their experience. This is because astral Projection occurs outside of conscious awareness and therefore cannot be recalled in the same way a regular dream or memory would be recalled. However, studying historical accounts of astral Projection can still give us valuable insights into this phenomenon despite these difficulties.

In conclusion, the history of astral Projection is long and varied. It has been described in texts worldwide, dating back thousands of years. While many of these accounts cannot be verified, they still provide us with valuable information about how different cultures have viewed this phenomenon.

Astral Projection and Lucidity

Astral Projection is the ability to consciously leave your body and explore the astral plane. This is done through various methods, including meditation, visualization, and specific breathing techniques. When you can astral project, you will be simultaneously aware of both your physical and spiritual bodies.
Astral Projection can be an incredibly powerful tool for personal growth and exploration. Lucid dreaming is a state in which you are aware that you are dreaming while you are asleep. You may be able to control the dreamscape and direct the dream's plot. Lucid dreaming can also occur during an out-of-body experience or Astral Projection.

Many people find that combining lucidity with astral Projection amplifies the experience and allows for greater exploration. In this section, we will look at the relationship between lucidity and astral Projection and discuss what benefits each can bring to the other.

While lucid dreaming is a separate phenomenon from astral Projection, the two can be practiced together to maximize each practice's benefits.

When lucid during an Out-of-body Experience or astral Projection, you can control your dreamscape and choose the places you wish to visit or the things you wish to do. Lucid dreaming during a conscious or semi-conscious projection can help you gain more control over the experience and allow you to direct your dreamscape in whichever direction you wish to lead. This can be especially helpful if you have trouble navigating your projected environment. You will still be outside of your body at the time, but you will be able to direct the dreamscape and manipulate your environment according to your will. Lucidity during an out-of-body experience can also provide a greater sense of comfort as you will be able to control your environment, not feeling like forces outside of your control are controlling you. Having control over your environment will help you reduce your anxiety during any out-of-body experiences you may have.

Beyond the benefits of lucid dreaming, combining the two practices can lead to more profound changes in the mind and the body. When learning how to lucid dream, a person may overcome certain obstacles and confront fears they previously believed impossible. This can positively affect the psyche and result in greater confidence in their day-to-day lives. Additionally, learning to lucid dream may lead to more profound changes in one's lifestyle choices and habits. These changes can range from moving back in with family to changing career paths and pursuing new hobbies, as this new confidence often leads to a renewed sense of life purpose. Additionally, incorporating lucid dreaming techniques into astral projection practice can enhance the Out-of-body Experience and allow for greater exploration. This can help people connect with their subconscious and develop greater self-awareness and insight.

Both lucid dreaming and astral Projection offer powerful personal growth and exploration insights. By learning how each practice works and practicing them together, you can gain insight into your subconscious mind and better understand your motivations and fears.
Astral Projection is a powerful tool that can be used for personal growth and exploration. Lucid dreaming is a state in which you are aware of the dream while you are asleep and can control it. Lucid dreaming during an astral projection amplifies the experience.
Many different techniques can induce an astral projection or lucid dream state. Some common methods include meditation, visualization, and specific breathing exercises. It is important to find a method that works best for you and practice regularly. Once you have mastered the technique, there are endless possibilities for exploration!

Chapter 2: The Benefits of Astral Projection

Astral projection is an experience in which the individual's consciousness leaves the physical body and enters into an astral plane. The astral planes are said to be higher vibrational frequencies than that of the physical world and, as such, offer a different perspective and range of experiences. Those who have undergone an astral projection often report feeling a sense of peace, love, and joy, as well as increased creativity, mental clarity, and healing. In this chapter, we will explore some of the many benefits of practicing astral projection.

Overcoming Fear

One of the main benefits of astral projection is that it can help you overcome your fears. When you are on the astral plane, you will have the opportunity to confront your fears in a safe and secure environment.
This can be a very powerful experience that can help you let go of your fears for good. In addition, when you are on the astral plane, you will have access to knowledge and wisdom that can help you understand your fears from a higher perspective. This understanding can be very helpful in overcoming your fears permanently.

Finally, when you are on the astral plane, you will be surrounded by loving energy that can help you heal your fears at a deep level. This healing energy can also help to prevent your fears from returning in the future. As a result, you can easily overcome your fear of flying on an astral plane so you can finally travel again without worrying about your safety or comfort.

Astral Projection will help you overcome fear at a deep level. While on the astral plane, you can confront your fears in a safe and controlled environment. You will be able also to access your knowledge and wisdom about fear and its causes. You will be given the loving energy needed to fully overcome your fears. Facing your fears can change your way of life and your perception of life. Astral Projection is a powerful healing tool that can help you change your life on a deep level by facing your worst fears in a controlled way.

To ensure your astral projection experience will help you overcome fear, it is important to start your Astral Projection practice with positive intentions and a clear purpose in mind. Even if your intentions are positive, it is important to understand that this is a natural process constantly evolving and usually accompanied by intense emotions that can sometimes be painful or uncomfortable.

Improved Sleep Quality

Another great benefit of astral projection is that it can help to improve your sleep quality. This is because when you are on the astral plane, you can get in touch with your higher self. Your higher self is a part of you connected to the divine source of all knowledge and wisdom. As such, when you are in touch with your higher self, you will be able to receive guidance and clarity about any issues that are causing you distress or confusion. This clarity can help improve your sleep quality by relieving any stress or anxiety you may be feeling.

In addition, ,you will also be surrounded by loving energy when you are on the astral plane. This energy can help to promote deep relaxation and peace. As a result, you will be able to fall asleep more easily and stay asleep for longer. You may even find that you no longer need to take sleeping pills or use other sleep aids to get a good night's rest.

Finally, when you are on the astral plane, you will have access to a higher level of consciousness. This higher level of consciousness can help you resolve any unfinished business that may be causing you sleepless nights. For example, if you have been arguing with your partner before bed, you may find that when you reach the astral plane, you can see the situation from a different perspective and resolve the issue once and for all. As a result, practicing astral projection can help to improve your sleep quality in several ways.

It is important to note that while astral projection can help improve your sleep quality, it is not recommended for those suffering from insomnia. If you are having difficulty sleeping, it is best to consult a doctor or sleep specialist before attempting astral projection.

Stress Relief

Stress relief is another one of the great benefits of astral projection. When you are on the astral plane, you can leave your body behind and relax in a completely stress-free environment. This can be a very helpful experience if you are dealing with a lot of stress in your life.

In addition, when you are on the astral plane, you will have access to knowledge and wisdom that can help you understand

and release stress. Finally, when you are on the astral plane, you will be surrounded by loving energy that can help you heal your stress at a deep level. As a result, you can easily relieve your stress on an astral plane to finally relax and enjoy your life again.

It is interesting to note that some people report that they can access other planes of existence while on the astral plane. These planes have even higher vibrational frequencies than the astral plane. As such, they offer an even more relaxing and stress-free environment. If you find yourself on one of these higher planes, you may want to take advantage of the opportunity to explore and learn about this new environment.

Astral projection can provide you with the opportunity to relax and release your stress in a variety of ways. You can explore new environments, receive wisdom and knowledge, and surround yourself with loving energy. As a result, astral projection can be a very helpful tool for managing stress in your life.
To experience the benefits of astral projection, it is important to learn how to astral project safely.

Increased Creativity

One of the most common benefits of astral projection is increased creativity. This is likely because when we can step outside of our physical bodies and see things from a new perspective, we can better come up with new ideas.
Some people who have never experienced astral projection may be skeptical of this claim. Still, there are many reported cases of people who have had sudden bursts of creativity after an astral projection experience. One famous example is the artist William Blake, who claimed that all his drawings and poems were inspired by visions he saw while astral projecting. If you are someone who struggles with creative blocks, the astral

projection could be a way to finally break through and start creating again. It may not be easy at first, but with practice, you could find yourself accessing a new level of creativity that you never knew existed.

Creativity is not just about coming up with new ideas; it is also about finding new ways to solve problems. If you are facing a difficult situation in your life, astral projection can help you see it from a different perspective and come up with a creative solution that you would never have thought of before.

In our everyday lives, we are often limited by our biases and how we have been conditioned to think. Astral projection can help us break free from these limitations and explore different ways of thinking that we may never have considered before. This can be especially helpful if you are stuck in a rut and feel like you will never be able to get out. By seeing things from a new perspective, you may finally be able to find a way out of the darkness and into the light.

One of the best ways to become more creative is to start practicing astral projection. The more you do it, the better you will become at it, and the more benefits you will start to see. If you are unsure where to start, many resources are available online that can help you learn astral projection basics. Once you have mastered the basics, you can start experimenting with different techniques and exploring ways to use astral projection to increase your creativity.

Astral projection is not just about increasing your creativity but also about expanding your consciousness and opening yourself up to new possibilities. When you can step outside your physical body and explore the astral plane, you are expanding your consciousness and opening yourself up to new dimensions of reality. This can be a transformative experience that can help you see the world in a new way.

If you are looking for a way to increase your creativity and open yourself up to new possibilities, astral projection is something you should consider. With practice, you can learn how to astral project at will and use it to explore different realms of existence. The possibilities are endless, and astral projection's benefits are vast.

Faster Learning

It is well documented that a person's capacity for learning is greatly enhanced when they are in an altered state of consciousness. This is because the conscious mind is relaxed during an altered state, and the subconscious mind is more open to receiving new information. When we are in a normal state of consciousness, the conscious mind is constantly active, filtering out any information it deems unnecessary. The subconscious mind is also constantly active, but it operates below the level of consciousness,, so we are unaware of its activity.

During an altered state of consciousness, the conscious mind is relaxed, and the subconscious mind is more accessible. This means new information can be passed from the subconscious to the conscious mind more easily. It has been shown that people who learn in an altered state of consciousness retain information better than those who learn in a normal state of consciousness. This is because the information bypasses the conscious mind and goes straight into the subconscious mind, where it can be stored more effectively. You can relax your conscious mind and allow your subconscious mind to absorb new information more easily. To learn effectively, it is important to have a clear intention and focus on what you want to learn. It is also important to be relaxed so that your mind is open to receiving new information.

Faster learning can be achieved through astral projection because:

• The conscious mind is relaxed, and the subconscious mind is more accessible.

• Information bypasses the conscious mind and goes straight into the subconscious mind.

• The subconscious mind can store information more effectively.

These three factors create an environment where new information can be learned quickly and easily.

Improved Physical Health

It is well documented that stress can hurt our physical health. Unfortunately, in today's fast-paced world, it's too easy to get caught up in the rat race and forget to take care of ourselves. This is where astral projection can be beneficial.
When we are stressed, our bodies go into fight-or-flight mode. This evolutionary response served us well when faced with genuine physical threats, but it's not so helpful when the threat is mental or emotional. When we're constantly in this state of high alert, our bodies produce more stress hormones, which can lead to many health problems, including high blood pressure, heart disease, and stroke.

Astral projection can help alleviate stress by providing a way to escape life's everyday pressures. When you astral project, you can visit any place you can imagine, including places of great beauty and peace. This can help calm and relax your mind and body and reduce the stress hormones circulating in your system.

In addition to reducing stress, there is evidence to suggest that astral projection can also improve physical health in other ways. For example, one study found that people who regularly astral projected had lower levels of pain after surgery than those who didn't.

It's thought that this is because when we astral project, we access a higher vibration frequency where pain doesn't exist. This higher frequency can also help to promote healing in the physical body. There are many accounts of people using astral projection to heal from serious illnesses.

So if you're looking for a way to improve your physical and mental and emotional wellbeing, the astral projection could be worth exploring. Astral projection is a powerful tool that can help you achieve your goals and live healthier, happier lives.

Exploration of new worlds

One of the most interesting things you can do with astral projection is exploring other worlds. This can be done in several ways. The first is to simply ask your spiritual guides to take you somewhere. This could be to another planet, dimension, or even just another part of the astral plane. Once you've made the request, you must relax and let them take you there. This is one of the best ways to explore another place because you'll already be in a relatively relaxed and calm state of mind, allowing you to go further and faster than you normally would be capable of going while awake.

You can also travel to locations you have seen before while dreaming or having lucid Out-of-body Experiences. This is perfect if you already have a vivid imagination and can take whatever form you want during your astral travels. This freedom is not limited to the astral plane either; it can also be used on the physical plane while you are awake through a process called lucid dreaming.

Traveling on the astral plane is often compared to lucid dreaming, but they are different experiences. While lucid dreaming is mostly a conscious activity, astral projection is a subconscious activity that requires you to calm down and detach from your body to happen. However, once you're detached from your physical body, you can return to it at will. While lucid dreaming is primarily an awareness exercise, your awareness expands while you're doing an Out-of-body Experience.

You can go through doorways between worlds during your astral projection travels. Doorways generally open naturally, but they can be created by telekinesis or focusing your attention on the door itself. The doorway is like a gateway that allows you to move from one location to another with a different set of rules or laws.

The second way to explore other worlds is to use your imagination. This is similar to lucid dreaming, except that you'll be conscious and aware that you're doing it. Simply close your eyes and imagine yourself in another place. It can be as simple as picturing yourself on a beach or in a forest. Once you have the image in your mind, start exploring it. Pay attention to every detail and try to interact with your surroundings as much as possible.

The third way to explore other worlds is to find a portal. These are usually located in natural places like forests or mountains. They can also be found in man-made places like temples or churches. To find a portal, simply ask your guides to show you one. Then, when you see it, walk through it without hesitation. You may find that you've been transported to a different part of the astral plane or even another planet.

No matter how you explore other worlds, the benefits are substantial. Not only will you gain a greater understanding of your spirituality, but you'll also be able to explore new landscapes and cultures. You'll also be able to heal from trauma and grief and develop stronger relationships with your spiritual guides. So whatever method you choose, be sure to reap the benefits of astral projection.

Heal from trauma

Trauma can be a very debilitating experience, both physically and mentally. Often, it can feel like the trauma is never-ending and that there is no way to escape it. However, it is possible to confront and heal from trauma through astral projection.

When confronted with a traumatic experience, our mind automatically goes into survival mode and shuts down. This is an innate coping mechanism that helps us to survive in difficult situations. However, this shutdown can also prevent us from effectively processing and dealing with the trauma. As a result, the trauma can become trapped in our subconscious mind, leading to flashbacks, nightmares, anxiety, and depression.

The good news is that we can access our subconscious mind through astral projection and address the trauma head-on. This process can be very confronting, but it is also incredibly healing.

By working through the trauma in astral form, we can release it from our subconscious mind and finally start to heal.

There are many different ways to heal from trauma through astral projection. One method is to simply revisit the traumatic event in astral form. This can help us understand what happened and why it affected us deeply. It can also help us realize that we are no longer in danger and are safe now.

Another method is to meet with our higher selves or guides in astral form. These beings can offer us guidance and understanding about what we are going through. They can also help us release the fear and pain associated with the trauma.

Finally, we can use astral projection to go to a place of peace and healing. This could be a beautiful garden or a peaceful beach. Alternatively, we could go to a place with personal meaning. For example, if we grew up near a forest, we might go there to find peace and solace. Wherever we choose to go, the important thing is that it provides us with a sense of calm and peace.

No matter which method we choose, the goal is always the same – to work through the trauma so we can finally start healing. By using astral projection, we can access parts of ourselves that have been hidden for far too long. As a result, we can begin to live our lives more fully and joyfully than ever before

Heal from Grief

Grief is a powerful emotion that can profoundly affect our lives. While it is natural to feel sadness and pain after losing a loved one, some people find it difficult to cope with their grief. This can lead to feelings of isolation, depression, and anxiety.

When we lose a loved one, it is natural to feel grief. Grief is a deep and powerful emotion that can sometimes feels overwhelming. While it is a normal and natural part of the healing process, it can also be very difficult to deal with.

Astral projection can be a helpful tool for those who are grieving. It can provide a way to connect with the deceased and offer closure and understanding. It can also help to release negative emotions and allow for inner peace. Astral projection can be an effective way to deal with grief. By leaving your body and exploring the astral planes, you can gain a new perspective on life and death. This can help you to accept the loss of your loved one and start to move on.

There are many different ways to grieve. Some people may find comfort in talking about their loss, while others may prefer to keep their feelings to themselves. There is no right or wrong way to grieve. However, astral projection may be worth considering if you find it difficult to cope with your grief. If you are struggling with grief, consider using astral projection to help you heal. It could be the key to finding the peace and understanding you need to move on.

For example, some people may notice that when they project their soul is in a state of fear or anxiety, this can often relate to childhood trauma or unresolved emotions that were suppressed during infancy and early childhood and which resurfaced during a bout of grief and bereavement. However, by projecting and meditating upon the astral plane and connecting with the loved ones on the other side one can often feel a sense of relief and expression.

Some people may even find that, by projecting to their dead relatives, they can gain new insight into how their relatives would have resolved any lingering issues; over time they can resolve these themselves or with the help of a therapist or counselor.

With all of these benefits, it's no wonder that more and more people are interested in learning about and practicing astral projection. If you're looking to improve your sleep quality, creativity, physical health, or just want to explore new worlds, astral projection may be right for you.

Chapter 3: Preparing for Your First Astral Projection Experience

Astral projection is an exciting and sometimes mysterious experience that can be enjoyed by anyone interested in exploring their spiritual side. However, before you embark on your first astral projection, you must create the perfect environment for the experience. This includes pulling together all the elements necessary to allow your mind to free itself from its physical constraints.

There are many ways to achieve this environment tailored to your specific needs and goals. This chapter will cover four key components necessary for a successful astral projection: creating the right mindset, developing relaxation techniques, clearing your mind, and finally setting yourself up for success.

However, before you begin any of these steps, it is important to understand some basic concepts about astral projection. This includes understanding what consciousness is, how astral projection works, and what conditions are necessary for the experience. We will also explore some common misconceptions about astral projection and provide tips on reducing anxiety before your first attempt.

Creating the Right Environment:

One of the most important factors in preparing for an astral project is setting yourself up for success. This section will discuss four key aspects of creating an optimal environment for astral projection:
- Mental preparation
- Setting guidelines for behavior and thoughts
- Creating sacred space and attracting positive energy

Mental Preparation:

The first step in creating a successful astral projection is mentally preparing yourself for the experience. This includes relieving any anxiety or stress associated with the proposed venture and focusing your thoughts on positive goals and objectives. Doing so will increase the likelihood of having a positive astral experience. Additionally, it is important to develop a strong belief in your ability to Astral project and put forth 100% effort during your experiment. Failure should not be an option!

Setting Guidelines for Behavior and Thoughts:

To maximize your chances of success during an astral projection, it is important to adhere to set guidelines regarding behavior and thoughts. These guidelines should be determined by both your conviction and those around you who may have more experience with astral projection. The most important guideline is to keep your mind clear at all times - no matter what happens during your trip! Following these guidelines will help reduce overall stress levels while en route and upon return home. Additionally, it is helpful to establish short-term, medium-term, and long-term goals while projecting to stay on track. These goals can be accomplished through visualization or focused thinking exercises before departure.

Creating a Sacred Space:

No matter how experienced you are with astral projection, ritualizing beforehand will always increase success rates overall. Creating a sacred space allows you to enter a mentally safe place where you can focus on Divine purpose without distraction or fear of negative outcomes. This space should be decorated with symbols or images that represent peace, love, trust, and self-care. It is also helpful to meditate or take another relaxant before beginning any meditation or visualization session to ease into a trance-like state. For best results, maintain awareness throughout the entire process by paying attention both consciously & subconsciously!

Attracting Positive Energy:

When seeking guidance from Higher Power during an astral projection, it is important to visualize it as clearly as possible so that communication may occur. It is also beneficial to surround yourself with supportive people who share similar spiritual values. By doing so, you are helping create an energetically conducive environment that will facilitate positive outcomes while projecting.

The Power of Belief

No matter how many years someone has been projecting, achieving success is impossible without first believing it is possible. This level of conviction allows your mind to be open to new experiences and possibilities. Additionally, when you are clear about your goals for projection, it becomes easier for Higher Power to guide you on your path.

There are many ways to develop a stronger belief in oneself. For example, reading about other people's success stories or speaking with those who have had positive experiences with Astral projection can increase your confidence that it is possible for you as well. Many books and websites offer tips, tricks, and guidance on the subject. However, the most important way to develop conviction is through trial and error - by trying different techniques and learning from your own experiences. The more you attempt astral projection and have positive results, the stronger your belief will become.

Relaxation Techniques

For an individual to succeed in astral projection, their physical body needs to be in a state of deep relaxation. This can be difficult for some because the process of achieving this state can be taxing in and of itself! Various methods can be employed to reach deep relaxation, such as progressive muscle relaxation, autogenic, and yoga Nidra.
Some find it helpful to combine different techniques to achieve optimal results. For example, progressive muscle relaxation can be used in conjunction with autogenic or yoga Nidra to further the relaxation process. It is also helpful to engage in these activities regularly to train your body to enter into a state of deep relaxation more easily. Doing so will increase the likelihood of success during your next Astral projection attempt!

Clearing Your Mind

One of the most difficult aspects of astral projection is clearing your mind completely before departure. This step is essential because any residual thoughts or emotions will be carried over into the astral realm and can potentially impact the quality of your experience. Many ways to achieve this include meditation, visualization, and focused thinking exercises.

Meditation:

The practice of meditation is an effective way to quiet the mind and focus on the present moment. This can be accomplished through various techniques such as mindfulness meditation, mantra meditation, or guided visualization. . The key is to find a method that works best for you and stick with it! Regular practice will train your mind to quiet itself more easily, which will come in handy during an astral projection attempt.

Visualization:

Visualization is another powerful tool that can be used to clear the mind and focus on desired outcomes. This technique involves picturing oneself in peaceful surroundings or achieving a specific goal. . The key is to focus on positive imagery that brings you joy while keeping all negative thoughts at bay. Doing so will increase the likelihood of having a successful astral projection experience!
Focused Thinking Exercises:
Assuming a relaxed position, either lying down or sitting comfortably, begin by taking several deep breaths through your nose and out through your mouth. Once you feel calm and collected, begin thinking about a topic or question you want clarity on. It is important not to allow any other thoughts to

enter your mind during this exercise – just focus on the question. After several minutes, open your eyes and journal any thoughts, feelings, or insights that came up for you during the exercise. Be sure not to force anything – just let whatever comes up naturally flow onto the page.

Retrieving Information from the Astral Realm

Now that you have mentally and physically prepared for astral projection, it is time to focus on what you would like to accomplish during your experience. This can be anything from exploring different environments to receiving guidance from Higher Power. The possibilities are endless!

When formulating your goals, it is important to be as specific as possible to increase the likelihood of achieving them. For example, rather than seeing your deceased grandfather during an astral projection, ask to see him in a particular place or doing a specific activity. The more specific you are, the easier for him to appear to you in the astral realm.
Writing down your goals before beginning the projection process is also helpful. This will remind you of what you are trying to achieve and help keep you focused during the experience. Additionally, it is important to trust that whatever information comes through during an astral projection is for your highest good – even if it doesn't make sense at the moment.

Returning Home Safely

Once you have accomplished your goals in the astral realm, it is time to return home. The most important thing to remember is not to resist or fight against the return process – this will only prolong your stay in the astral realm and make it more difficult to return home. Instead, just relax and let yourself be drawn back into your physical body. It is also helpful to visualize yourself surrounded by white light during this process to protect yourself from negative energy.

Upon returning home, it is important to take some time to ground yourself and adjust back to physical reality. This can be done by eating something grounding such as root vegetables, spending time outside in nature, or taking a hot bath. It is also helpful to journal your experience afterward to process any insights or information received during the projection.

Dealing with Setbacks

It is important to remember that not every astral projection will be successful. There will be times when you cannot achieve a deep state of relaxation or clear your mind completely. These setbacks are normal and should not discourage you from continuing to explore this amazing experience!

When dealing with setbacks, it is helpful to take a step back and analyze what went wrong. This will allow you to correct mistakes and increase the likelihood of success during your next attempt. Additionally, it is important to be patient with yourself and trust that you will eventually be able to achieve your goals. After all, practice makes perfect!

Conclusion

Astral projection is an exciting and often mystical experience that can be enjoyed by anyone interested in exploring their spiritual side. However, before embarking on your first astral projection, creating the perfect environment for the experience is important. This includes mentally preparing yourself, developing relaxation techniques, clearing your mind, and setting guidelines for behavior and thoughts. Doing so will increase the likelihood of having a positive and productive astral projection experience!

Chapter 4: Main Steps of Astral Projection

Have you ever wanted to explore the cosmos, or visit distant lands without having to leave your body behind? If so, then astral projection may be for you. Astral projection is an age-old practice that allows individuals to separate their consciousness from their physical bodies and explore the world around them in a non-physical form.

While astral projection can be done spontaneously, it often takes some planning and preparation in order to achieve a successful outcome. This chapter will teach you everything you need to know about astral projection, from the initial stages of preparation to the moment you finally leave your body behind. With this knowledge at your disposal, you'll be well on your way to discovering the mysteries of the astral realm.

The Body Falls Asleep

The first step in astral projection is to ensure that your physical body is asleep. This may seem like a difficult task if you're used to falling asleep naturally, but there are some things you can do to make it happen. One method is to relax your whole body starting with your toes and working your way up. Once your entire body is relaxed, begin focusing on your breath and count each inhale and exhale until you eventually drift off into sleep. It's important not to force yourself to sleep, as this can lead to frustration and ultimately hinder your efforts. Just let it happen naturally and before long, you'll find yourself in a deep slumber.

The conscious mind is aware, but the body is asleep

Now that your body is asleep, it's time for your conscious mind to take over. You'll still be aware of your surroundings and what's happening around you, but your physical body will be completely unresponsive. It's important not remain focused on any one thing for too long, as this can cause you to lose focus and drift back into unconsciousness. Instead, allow your mind to wander and explore whatever comes into it. The key at this stage is to remain calm and Relaxed, as any sort of anxiety or stress will only make it more difficult to achieve astral projection.

The conscious mind and body are both awake

At this point, both your conscious mind and physical body should be awake and alert. It's now time to begin the process of actually leaving your body behind. There are many different methods you can use to achieve this, but one of the most effective is known as the rope technique. To begin, imagine yourself standing at the edge of a cliff overlooking a vast landscape below. Now imagine a rope extending from the ground all the way up to where you're standing. Grab hold of the rope and start lowering yourself down slowly until eventually, you feel yourself becoming separated from your physical body. Once this happens, simply let go of the rope and allow yourself to float away into the astral realm.

Transitioning into the astral realm

As soon as you've let go of the rope , you'll find yourself in the astral realm. This realm exists beyond our physical world and is said to be populated by all sorts of beings, both good and bad. It's important not to focus on any one thing for too long at this stage, as doing so can cause you headaches or dizziness. Instead, just take in your surroundings and familiarize yourself with this new environment. After a while, you'll start getting used to it and transitioning into the astral realm will become easier than ever before.

Moving around the Astral Realm

Now that you're familiar with your surroundings, it's time to start moving around. The astral realm is vast and there's no shortage of things to see and explore. However, it's important not to get too caught up in the beauty of this place. Remember, you're here for a reason and it's important to stay focused on your goal.

One way to move around in the astral realm is by simply thinking about where you want to go. The astral realm is highly malleable and will take on whatever form you desire. So if you want to visit a certain location or person, all you need to do is Picture it in your mind and you'll be transported there instantaneously. Another way to move around is by using your body. Just like in the physical world, you can use your legs to walk or your arms to fly. The possibilities are endless, so feel free to experiment and find what works best for you.

Communication in the Astral Realm

One of the most interesting aspects of the astral realm is the fact that you can communicate with other beings that reside there. This is done through what's known as telepathy, or the ability to communicate without using words. In order to communicate with someone in the astral realm, simply focus your thoughts on them and they'll receive your message. It's important not to force the communication, as this can result in frustration on both ends. Just let it happen naturally and before long, you'll be having full-fledged conversations with other astral beings.

Returning to your Physical Body

At some point, you'll likely want to return to your physical body. There's no set time limit on how long you can remain in the astral realm, but it's important not to overdo it. After all, there's a reason you decided to leave your body behind in the first place and there's no need to drag out your experience any longer than necessary.

When you're ready to return, simply focus your thoughts on your physical body and you'll find yourself back inside it in no time. It's important not to resist this process, as doing so can lead to complications. Just let it happen naturally and before you know it, you'll be back in the physical world once again.

Tips for Successful Astral Projection

The following tips will help ensure that your astral projection experience is a successful one:
- **Practice regularly**: The more often you practice astral projection, the easier it will become. Just like anything else, regular practice will lead to improved results.
- **Keep a journal**: Recording your experiences in a journal is a great way to track your progress and remember what worked well during previous attempts.
- **Find a comfortable place**: It's important to find a comfortable place to relax both your mind and body before beginning the astral projection process. Otherwise, you may find it difficult to achieve success.
- **Focus on your breath**: Focusing on your breath is a great way to relax your mind and body and prepare for astral projection.
- **Set an intention**: Before beginning the astral projection process, take a moment to set an intention for what you hope to achieve during your experience. This can help keep you focused throughout the process.
- **Visualize success**: Throughout the astral projection process , visualize yourself achieving success. This positive visualization can help increase the likelihood of an successful outcome.

Pitfalls to Avoid During Astral Projection

There are a few potential pitfalls that can occur during astral projection, but the good news is that they're all avoidable. By being aware of these potential dangers, you can help ensure that your experience is a positive one. Some of the pitfalls to avoid include:

- **Losing focus**: It's important to remain focused throughout the entire astral projection process. If you lose focus at any point, you may find yourself back in your physical body without even realizing it.
- **Getting lost**: The astral realm is vast and there's no shortage of things to see and explore. However, it's important not to get so caught up in your surroundings that you forget why you're there in the first place. Otherwise, you may find it difficult to return to your physical body.
- **Communicating with negative entities**: There are both good and bad entities in the astral realm. It's important to avoid communicating with negative entities, as they may try to lure you away from your physical body or even harm you in some way.
- **Trying too hard**: It's important not to force the astral projection process, as this can lead to frustration and ultimately hinder your efforts. Just relax and let it happen naturally and before long, you'll find yourself in the astral realm.

Frequently Asked Questions about Astral Projection

Astral projection is often shrouded in mystery, which can make it difficult to know what to expect. Here are answers to some of the most commonly asked questions about astral projection:
- **Is astral projection dangerous?:** There's no need to worry about astral projection being dangerous. It's a natural phenomenon that we're all capable of doing.

However, there are a few potential pitfalls that could occur if you're not careful.

- **What happens if I get lost in the astral realm?:** If you find yourself getting lost in the astral realm, simply focus your thoughts on your physical body and you'll find yourself back inside it in no time. There's no need to worry about getting permanently stuck in the astral realm, as it's impossible for that to happen.
- **How do I know if I'm doing it right?:** There's no one right or wrong way to do astral projection. Everyone experiences it differently, so there's no need to worry about whether or not you're doing it right. Just relax and let it happen naturally and you'll be fine.
- **Can everyone do it?:** Yes! Astral projection is something that we're all capable of doing. However, some people may find it easier than others due to factors such as regular practice, natural ability, etc.

Astral projection is an amazing ability that allows us to explore the world beyond our physical bodies. By following the steps outlined in this guide, you'll be well on your way to experiencing the astral realm for yourself. Just remember to relax and have fun with it, as there's no need to worry about doing it perfectly. Everyone experiences astral projection differently, so there's no right or wrong way to do it. Just let it happen naturally and before you know it, you'll be exploring the astral realm in no time.

Chapter 5: Your First Time in the Astral Realm

Have you ever wondered what it would be like to explore the astral realm? This dimension exists beyond the physical world and teems with energy, creativity, and mystical experiences. This chapter will explore what you can expect when you venture into the astral realm for the first time. We will also guide how to navigate this ethereal space and offer tips on returning to your physical body.

What to Expect

When you enter the astral realm, it appears very similar to the physical world. The main difference is that everything is made of energy instead of matter. You may see people or beings made of light and geometric shapes and patterns. It is also possible to encounter deceased loved ones or other spiritual guides.

As you explore the astral realm, you will notice that your thoughts and emotions directly impact your surroundings. If you focus on negative thoughts, you may be in a dark and scary place.

However, if you focus on positive thoughts, you will be surrounded by light and love. The astral realm is a creative space, so you can use your imagination to manifest anything you desire. You may also find that your psychic abilities are greatly enhanced in the astral realm.

This is because your energy can flow freely between both worlds. At this journey stage, focus your energy on healing yourself through meditation. Try experimenting with different breathing techniques or simply listen to calming music or sounds of nature.

Try to clear your mind of all distractions and focus only on your breath and the flow of your energy within your body. This will help you to heal any physical or emotional issues that you may have experienced in your life.
Once you have reached a state of deep relaxation, focus on your third eye, and imagine a beam of pure white light flowing down from it towards your heart chakra. This light will act as a transmission button for the Akashic Records and allow your spiritual self to communicate with your physical self deeper.
As a result, your psychic abilities will become much stronger over time, and you can communicate with the spirit world without much effort. Suddenly you will be shown many different scenes. These scenes relate to your life and the lessons you need to learn to progress as a spiritual being.

How to Navigate the Astral Realm

The astral realm is an ethereal space beyond the physical world. It is a dimension of pure energy where thoughts and emotions directly impact your surroundings. Focusing on positive thoughts and emotions is important to navigating the astral realm. This will help you to create your own reality within this space. You may find yourself attracted to certain areas or beings as you explore the celestial realm.
These places or beings will offer you guidance and support on your journey. Follow your intuition and trust that you are being guided towards your highest good. If you find yourself in a dark or negative space, simply focus on your breath and imagine yourself surrounded by white light. This light will protect you from harm and guide you back to the positive area of the astral realm.

It is important to focus on your third eye chakra to return to your physical body. Imagine a beam of light flowing down from this chakra and into your heart chakra. This will help align your energy bodies and allow you to transition back into the physical world.

The conscious mind and body are both awake.

When you enter the astral realm, your conscious mind and body may awake. This means that you will be aware of both worlds simultaneously. You may see through your physical body's eyes while also experiencing the astral realm in all its glory.

If this happens, it is important to focus on your breath and try to relax as much as possible. It is also helpful to focus on one thing at a time, so you don't become overwhelmed by all the different stimuli around you.
For example, if you are looking at your physical body from the heavenly realm, focus on one thing at a time, such as the movement of your chest as you breathe or the feeling of your clothes against your skin.

By focusing on one thing at a time, you will gradually become more accustomed to this experience and can relax fully without becoming overwhelmed. Suppose your conscious mind and body are both awake. In that case, it is also possible to use this experience to heal any physical or emotional issues you may have experienced.
Simply focus on your breath and imagine yourself surrounded by white light. This light will flow into any areas of your body that need healing and will help to release any negativity or pain

you may be holding onto. You can also use this light to fill up empty spaces within yourself, so you feel whole again.

Transitioning into the Astral Realm

There are many different ways that people can transition into the astral realm. Some people use specific breathing techniques or meditation to induce an out-of-body experience. Others may use psychedelic drugs such as DMT to reach an altered state of consciousness where they can access the astral realm.

However, it is also possible to transition into this dimension without using any external aids at all. To do this, simply focus on relaxing your whole body as much as possible until you reach a state of deep relaxation. Once you have reached this state, focus on your third eye chakra, and imagine a beam of white light flowing down into your heart chakra.
Continue to focus on this light while your thoughts slowly drift away into a state of deep relaxation. After some time, you will find yourself drifting out of your body and into the astral realm, where you will be able to travel freely throughout this area until a point in time when you feel the need to return to your body.
As a result, you will be taken into the astral realm, where you can explore all kinds of different realities depending on your thoughts, emotions, and intentions. You can use your psychic abilities to tap into the Akashic Records at any time by entering your third eye chakra and visualizing white light connecting your physical body to your spiritual body. This spiritual light will then transmit your thoughts into the realm of the Akashic Records, where you can view your past and current life as you live it.

Once you are transported to the Akashic Records, you may communicate with many different Guides and other beings connected to the Akashic Records realm.

Searching for your Higher Self

After settling into the astral realm, you may search for your higher self. This part of you exists on a higher frequency and contains all your spiritual knowledge and wisdom. Finding your higher self can help you remember who you are and why you are here on this earth.
To find your higher self, focus on your breath and imagine yourself surrounded by white light.
This light will lift you into the higher dimensions, where you can meet with your higher self. Once you have found your higher self, they will be able to give you any information you need to remember your true identity and purpose in this lifetime.

If you feel lost or confused at any point during your journey, simply ask your higher self for guidance, and they will be more than happy to help you.

Your higher self is always available to you and can be accessed at any time, regardless of where you are or what you are doing. Simply focus on your breath and imagine yourself surrounded by white light. This light will take you to the higher dimensions, where you can meet with your higher self and receive the guidance and support you need. It is important to remember that your higher self loves you unconditionally and will always be there for you, no matter what. You can always rely on them to help you remember who you are and why you are here on this earth.

Meeting Your Animal Guides

You may meet with different animal guides as you explore the astral realm. These guides can take many forms, such as lions, tigers, eagles, dolphins, etc.

Animal guides offer us guidance and support on our journey through life. They can help us connect with our animal instincts and teach us how to live in harmony with nature. Trust that whatever form they take, they are here to help you in whatever way they can.

If an animal guide appears to you in the astral realm, simply focus on your breath and imagine yourself surrounded by white light. This light will protect you from any harm and help connect you with this guide on a deeper level. Once you have established this connection, ask them any questions about life or your journey specifically.

They will be more than happy to answer any questions and give you the guidance and support you need to move forward on your path. Remember that animal guides are always available to us, even when we don't realize it. They can communicate with us through our dreams or by appearing physically in our lives when we least expect it.

Trust that they are always there for us, even when we can't see them.

Discovering Your Life Purpose

One of the best ways to explore the astral realm is by using your imagination. This dimension is full of energy and creativity, so you can use your imagination to manifest anything you desire.

As you explore the astral realm, pay attention to any images, symbols, or messages you see. These images may contain clues about your life purpose or the lessons you need to learn in this lifetime. If you focus on these clues, they will help to guide you on your path. Connecting with different guides who can offer you support and guidance on your journey is possible.

This light will take you to the higher dimensions, where you can meet with these guides and receive their message for you.

Your life purpose is always available to you, even when you don't realize it. It is encoded in your soul and is waiting to be discovered by you. The best way to discover your life purpose is by using your imagination and following the clues presented to you along the way. Trust that everything happens for a reason and that there is a greater plan at work, even if you can't see it right now.

Exploring Your Past Lives

The astral realm is a dimension of pure energy where thoughts and emotions directly impact your surroundings. In this realm, it is possible to explore your past lives.
This can be a healing experience as it can help you understand why you are facing certain challenges in this lifetime. It can also help you remember your connection to all of humanity and the interconnectedness of all souls.
Explore your past lives, focus on your breath, and imagine yourself surrounded by white light. This light will take you into the higher dimensions, where you can access the Akashic Records. These records contain all the information about every

soul that has ever existed. Once you are in the Akashic Records, ask to see any past lives relevant to your current life situation. It is also possible to ask for guidance from your guides or other beings connected to the Akashic Records realm.

These beings will be able to give you any information that you need to help you make better decisions in your life and will be able to guide you if you feel as though you are lost or confused about what to do next in your life.

Return to Your Body

When you are ready to return to your physical body, simply focus on your third eye chakra and imagine a beam of white light flowing down from it into your heart chakra. This will help align your energy bodies and allow you to transition back into the physical world. It is also important to focus on your breath and relax as much as possible.

This will help to release any negative emotions or thoughts you may have picked up while in the astral realm. Simply let go of anything that is no longer serving you and trust that you are being guided back to your body for a reason. Everything happens for a reason, and there is always a greater plan at work, even if we can't see it right now.

In this chapter, we have explored what you can expect when you venture into the astral realm for the first time. We have also guided how to navigate this ethereal space and offered tips on returning to your physical body.

Chapter 6: Overcoming Obstacles to Astral Projecting

Everyone has experienced some form of an obstacle while trying to achieve a goal. For some, finding ways to overcome these obstacles is easy and continue with what they were trying to do. However, these obstacles can seem impossible for others, causing them to give up altogether. The same can be said for those who are trying to astral project. While astral projection has many benefits, the process is not without its challenges. In this chapter, we will explore some of the most common obstacles people face when trying to astral project and provide tips on how to overcome them.

Fear

Fear is one of the most common obstacles people face when trying to astral project. This is understandable since it involves leaving your physical body behind and venturing into the unknown. However, there are many ways to overcome this fear and successfully astral project.

One way to overcome fear is to simply face it. Recognize that you are afraid and then try to understand why. Once you know what is causing your fear, you can begin to work on overcoming it. Often, the fear of astral projection is based on a lack of understanding or misinformation. Learning more about the process and what to expect can help to ease your fears. It can also help you understand what parts of astral projection might frighten you, so you can take control of them or learn how to manage them better. You can overcome the fear of exploring your astral body in many ways – meditation, hypnosis, reading about the process, talking about it with others, or watching others explore the astral plane and report their experiences.

Another way to reduce fear is to take baby steps. If leaving your body scares you, start by just visualizing yourself doing so. See yourself floating outside of your body and then gently returning inside. Try to visualize and imagine your body floating out of it and exploring it as much as possible and as often as possible. Eventually, this will become easier, and your chances of successfully projecting will increase greatly as you become accustomed to the process and know what to expect.

Some people find it helpful to get a guide to help them get out of their bodies before trying to project on their own. This can be a spirit guide or someone experienced in astral projection who knows how to effectively guide you out of your body and onto the astral plane when you are ready for it to happen.

You may also find that talking with a therapist or minister can be very helpful in overcoming fears about astral projection and pulling them off the plane. Talking with another person about your fears and thought processes can help you realize that you are not alone in experiencing them and can lead you to find a healthy way to deal with them so that you can explore your celestial body healthily and safely.

Practice this regularly until you feel comfortable enough to move on to the next step.

Once you are ready, try projecting a short distance at first. For example, see yourself moving from one side of the room to the other. Or visualize yourself flying high above the ground. Slowly increase the distance as you become more confident with the process. Eventually, with the practice and guidance of a trustworthy spirit guide, you can learn how to control your astral body and travel great distances simply by willing it to happen and controlling your movements with your mind. There are various methods to astral project and many different ways to do it, so take your time and practice until you master the best method.

It is also important to remember that you are in control at all times during astral projection. You can always return to your body if you feel uncomfortable or scared. Knowing that you have this safety net can help ease any fears about venturing too far from your body.

Doubt

Doubt is often the main obstacle to astral projection. Many people doubt whether the astral projection is even possible, and if it is possible, they may doubt whether they can do it themselves. It is important to remember that astral projection is a natural ability that we all have. Doubting that you can do it can prevent you from being able to do it. Doubt is destructive to learning a new skill such as astral projection because when you question whether you can do something, you tend to unconsciously block off learning how to do it. When you consciously block off learning a new skill, you effectively block off that ability to learn and become an expert in that skill, thus limiting your potential in life and sabotaging your successes.

If you find yourself doubting whether or not astral projection is possible or whether you can do it, try to remember some of the evidence that suggests that astral projection is real. There are many accounts of people who have had spontaneous astral projections and accounts of people who have deliberately induced astral projection through different methods. If so many people can do it, there must be something. Additionally, scientific studies suggest that astral projection is a real phenomenon. For example, some studies have found that people who claim to have experienced astral projection show changes in brain activity during the experience.

Once you doubt the reality of astral projection, you can then move on to doubting whether or not you can do it yourself. Remember that everyone has the ability to astral project – it is simply a matter of learning how to do it. Whether you can do this on your own or under someone else's guidance is up to you to decide, but remember that being guided through the process is not necessarily a barrier since you can learn much by being taught by someone more experienced than you in astral projection. Many different methods can be used to induce astral projection, and many resources can teach you how to do it.
If you dedicate yourself to learning how to astral project, there is no reason why you cannot achieve success.

Distractions

One of the most common obstacles to astral projecting is distractions. The mind is very good at finding things to focus on when we try to relax and let go. This can be anything from random thoughts to sounds in the environment to physical sensations. The most important tactic in preventing these distractions is to practice becoming more aware of your surroundings. Once you learn how to become relaxed in the physical world, then you can begin practicing relaxing your physical body.

Once you have learned how to relax and put your physical body at ease, it's time to practice focusing energy on yourself. Begin by visualizing that part of your body you wish to work on and imagine it relaxing and loosening up. The next step is to carefully visualize releasing that energy and imagining it going into your "aura" and surrounding your body. Once you have released your aura and relaxed and let your body go, it is time to practice visualizing your aura and letting go of it. You will know that you have mastered this when you successfully let go of your aura and physical body all at once.

You can do a few things to try and overcome the obstacle of distractions. First, creating a space conducive to relaxation and concentration is important. This means finding a place where you will not be disturbed by others and where there are no distracting noises or bright lights. Once you have found a suitable space, you can begin to focus on your breathing. Taking deep, slow breaths will help your body to relax and will also help to clear your mind.

If you are still unable to relax enough to astral project, you can try practicing with a candle or object that burns slowly. As the smoldering candle or object glows and flickers, you can focus on this and imagine it lifting you out of your body and floating freely in the astral plane. This can help prepare you for the trip to your dream world and can help to teach you how to navigate the astral planes with your mind rather than your physical body. Another helpful method for overcoming distractions is visualization. Visualize yourself in a peaceful place, such as a beach or forest. Picture yourself surrounded by blue skies and green trees. Focus on the sensations of the environment, such as the sound of the waves or the smell of the flowers. Allow yourself to sink into this peaceful place until all other thoughts have faded away.

If you find that you are still struggling with distractions, there are several other techniques that you can try. Guided meditation recordings can be very helpful in providing distraction-free environments and helping you to relax deeply. There are also many books available on astral projection that can provide guidance and support.

Intense Emotions

Intense emotions can be both a blessing and a curse in astral projecting. On the one hand, having strong emotions can make it easier to leave your body and enter the astral plane. On the other hand, emotional turmoil can make it harder to focus and maintain concentration, two things essential for successful astral projection.

If you're feeling particularly emotional before attempting to astral project, it's important to find a way to calm yourself down. Relaxation techniques such as deep breathing or meditation can help manage stress and anxiety. Once you feel more relaxed and centered, your chances of successfully astral projecting will increase. This also helps keep your negative emotions under control and out of your body to avoid unnecessary conflict or conflict with your entity contact.

In some cases, intense emotions may be caused by entities on the astral plane. If you feel suddenly angry, afraid, or depressed for no apparent reason, you're possibly picking up on an entity's negative energy. In these cases, it's best to release the emotion and move on. Do not engage with the entity or allow yourself to get caught up in its negativity.

While intense emotions can be challenging when trying to astral project, they can also be used to your advantage. If you can harness your emotions and direct them towards your goal of astral projection, you may find it easier to achieve success. Use your emotions to fuel your visualization process and imagine yourself soaring through the astral planes with ease. With practice, you'll be able to overcome any obstacles standing in between you and successful astral projection.

Intense emotions can also be a good indication of strong psychic energy. If you have strong feelings for someone or something on the physical plane, the energy of your intense emotion can also manifest on the astral plane. If you encounter strong emotional energy while astral projecting, it's likely coming from an actual source on the astral plane. Do your best to be conscious of your emotions and use them for what they are: a powerful form of energy that can be used to strengthen your psychic abilities.

Sleep paralysis is characterized by muscle atonia and an inability to move or speak. It can occur during the transition between wakefulness and sleep or vice versa. Although it is usually brief, it can be quite horrifying, especially if you are unfamiliar with it.

There are two types of sleep paralysis: isolated and recurrent. Isolated sleep paralysis is a one-time event not associated with any other disorder. Recurrent sleep paralysis is when someone experiences multiple episodes of sleep paralysis over time. It can be associated with other disorders such as narcolepsy, anxiety, and depression.

There are several possible causes of sleep paralysis. It may be caused by a disruption in the normal sleep cycle, such as jet lag or shift work. Sleep deprivation can also trigger sleep paralysis. Other potential causes include using certain medications, alcohol abuse, and underlying medical conditions such as narcolepsy or migraines.

You can do a few things to reduce your risk of experiencing sleep paralysis:

1. Maintain a regular sleep schedule and get plenty of restful sleep.
2. Avoid using drugs or alcohol before bedtime.
3. If you have an underlying medical condition causing sleep paralysis, talk to your doctor about treatment options.

If you experience an episode of sleep paralysis, you can do a few things to ease your symptoms.

First, try to relax and focus on your breathing, then mentally will yourself to move your body or limbs. If you feel like you're going to panic, remind yourself that you are safe, and this is only temporary, then get up and move around once the episode has passed to help reenergize your body.

Sleep paralysis can be a frightening experience, but it is not dangerous and does not last long. Understanding what it is and how to cope with it can minimize its impact on your life.

Chapter 7: The Different Types of Astral Projection

There are different types of astral projection, each with its own unique characteristics. In this chapter, we will explore the different types of astral projection, including lucid dreams, out-of-body experiences, remote viewing, and near-death experiences.

Lucid Dreams.

A lucid dream is a type of dreaming during which the individual is aware that they are dreaming. Lucid dreams can occur spontaneously or may be induced through various techniques. During a lucid dream, the individual has a sense of control over their environment and may be able to manipulate the dream content.
Evidence suggests that lucid dreaming is a state of consciousness between wakefulness and sleep. There is increased brain activity in the frontal and temporal lOut-of-body Experience during lucid dreaming, similar to the brain activity seen during wakefulness. However, there are also similarities between lucid dreaming and sleep, as both states are associated with decreased activity in the prefrontal cortex.

There are many theories as to why people have lucid dreams. One theory suggests that lucid dreams are a way for the brain to process information and sort through memories. Another

theory posits that lucid dreaming is a way for the individual to practice skills or rehearse for future events. It has also been suggested that lucid dreaming may be a way for people to process emotions or work through traumas. Several techniques have been developed to encourage the occurrence of a lucid dream. For example, inducing sleep paralysis immediately before a person falls asleep may help individuals remember their dreams. A person in sleep paralysis suffers from the inability to move or speak while dreaming. This state can stimulate several REM periods during the night when a person is normally asleep, leading to vivid dreams.
Another technique involves performing reality checks before falling asleep and during a dream to remind an individual that they are still dreaming. Individuals with lucid dreams report experiencing a wide variety of dream scenarios, from traveling to visiting deceased family members.

The experience of a lucid dream differs among individuals. Some people experience vivid lucid dreams surrounded by the sounds and sights of the dream world. Others may be aware that they are dreaming yet unable to interact with the dream world at all or may be unable to control their dreams. It is also possible to experience a lucid dream without realizing it is occurring.
Lucid dreams can have both positive and negative consequences. On the positive side, lucidity allows for greater self-awareness and can be used as a tool for self-exploration. Lucid dreaming has also been used as a treatment for nightmares, as the individual can take control of the dream content and change it to something more pleasant. Conversely, lucid dreams can sometimes lead to sleep disorders such as insomnia. In addition, some individuals may find it difficult to return to normal consciousness after having a lucid dream, which can lead to fatigue and confusion.

Out-of-Body Experiences

Out-of-body experiences refer to occasions where people report feeling as though they have left their physical body and are observing it from the outside. Out-of-Body Experiences can happen spontaneously or may be induced through various techniques, such as meditation or sensory deprivation.
Individuals who experience Out-of-Body Experiences report feeling detached from their physical body and can often move around and interact with the physical environment while out of the body. Out-of-Body Experiences can be positive experiences such as spiritual experiences or revelations. Still, they can also be negative experiences such as feeling threatened or fearing for the physical body.

Studies suggest that Out-of-Body Experiences occur as a fringe of consciousness during dreams, and their ability to function while out of the body is dependent upon the depth of the dream experience. It is also possible to experience an out-of-body experience while in a "dream state" of sleep, which may explain the occurrence of such experiences under hypnosis or during sensory deprivation and meditation studies.
While out-of-body experiences have some benefits for those who have them, there are also potential risks. Individuals who experience out-of-body experiences may have trouble returning to their physical body and may experience confusion or disorientation. It is also suspected that people with out-of-body experiences may have a greater likelihood of experiencing sleep paralysis. The sense of detachment from the physical body could also increase the risk of physical injury while exploring the environment or attempting to interact with it.

Four main features usually characterize out-of-Body Experiences:

1) The feeling of leaving one's body
2) The ability to see one's own body from an external vantage point
3) The feeling of being located in space outside of one's body
4) The ability to move around in this space independently from one's physical body

People often report out-of-body experiences during times of extreme stress or danger, such as near-death experiences. It is thought that Out-of-Body Experiences may provide individuals with a way to cope with potentially life-threatening situations by allowing them to detach from their physical bodies. Sometimes, Out-of-Body Experiences have been associated with mystical or religious experiences.

There is some scientific evidence to support the existence of Out-of-Body Experiences. For example, studies have found that individuals who claim to have had an Out-of-Body Experience often show signs of verifiable neural activity during the experience. However, there is no definitive explanation for how or why Out-of-Body Experiences occur. Some scientists believe that they could be related to changes in brain chemistry or blood flow, while others think they may be caused by electrical stimulation of certain brain areas.

Remote Viewing

Remote Viewing is the ability to perceive and describe people, places, objects, or events at a distance, without using the five physical senses. This includes all forms of sense, including extrasensory perception such as clairvoyance and precognition. There are different types of Remote Viewing, but they all share the common element of using the mind to gather information about something that is not within physical sight or hearing range. The most common type of Remote Viewing is probably telepathy, which is the ability to receive thoughts from another person without them having to verbalize those thoughts.

Suppose an individual's mind is "tuned in" enough to pick up these telepathic thoughts. In that case, they can tap into the collective consciousness and view an image or history about another person or place. The most common example of Remote Viewing is ghost hunting, in which a person's paranormal abilities are used to view the spirits of the dead and communicate with the spiritual realm. Investigators often use remote Viewing in paranormal cases to help them determine where paranormal activity might be occurring or what types of spirits might be involved.

Some individuals have claimed to be able to view things remotely using the power of their mind and Extrasensory Perception to gather information about locations or situations without physically being at or near them.

Other types of Remote Viewing include:

- **Psychometry** .
- **Remote Viewing** .
- **Precognition** .

There is a long history of people claiming Remote Viewing abilities, going back to ancient times. In recent years, Remote Viewing has been studied scientifically, and there are some documented cases of people with this ability. The US military even had a program called Stargate Project in which people with Remote Viewing abilities were used for intelligence gathering purposes.

Despite all this, there is still much skepticism about Remote Viewing. Many people believe that it is impossible and that any claims of its existence must be fraudulent. There are several possible explanations for why this skepticism exists. Some people may simply not be open to the idea that there could be anything beyond what we can see and hear with our five physical senses. Others may be afraid of giving up their belief in a materialistic view of reality where everything that exists is physically tangible. And lastly, some people may be concerned about the ethical implications of using Remote Viewing for spying or other nefarious purposes.

Whatever the reason for skepticism, it is important to remember that just because something cannot be proven does not mean it doesn't exist. There are many things in the world that science has not been able to explain yet, and Remote Viewing could very well be one of them. It is also worth noting that even if Remote Viewing does exist, that doesn't mean it can't be misused, just like any other ability or technology. It is up to each individual to decide whether or not they believe in Remote Viewing and how they would use it if they did possess this ability.

Near-Death Experiences

Near-Death Experiences are one of the most well-known and controversial types of astral projection. Accounts of Near-Death Experiences have been recorded throughout history and in many cultures. Most often, people report having Near-Death Experiences during a period of unconsciousness or near death, such as when they are under anesthesia during surgery or when they are close to death due to an accident or illness.
People experiencing Near-Death Experiences often report seeing a tunnel or bright light, most commonly described as

being through darkness or nothingness. In most cases, people report feeling peaceful and calm during their Near-Death Experience, and many claim to feel nothing but unconditional love and acceptance during this experience. Many people also report their afterlife experiences as similar or identical to descriptions of Heaven and Hell in the Bible or other religious texts. Some people who experience Near-Death Experiences claim that they had returned to their physical body and healed from whatever illness or condition they suffered before they died.

People with Near-Death Experiences are often intensely concerned with sharing their stories with others, and some have set up websites to share their accounts in detail. These websites have generated a wide range of responses from the scientific community. Some scientists are skeptical of Near-Death Experiences and believe that they are more likely to result from hallucinations or stress than actual evidence of the afterlife. Other scientists, especially religious ones, claim that people can't enter a Near-Death Experience unless their physical life is ended and that Near-Death Experiences are proof of life after death.

Regardless of how one feels about Near-Death Experiences, it is important to note that they are an extremely common phenomenon. Many people report having Near-Death Experiences that are very similar to each other. Most people who have Near-Death Experiences do not deny having experienced these dreams or visions and claim that they had very real and profound experiences when they were in a Near-Death state.

Four main elements are typically reported in Near-Death Experiences:
1) A sense of peace and well-being

2) Out-of-body experiences
3) Meeting deceased loved ones
4) A life review

People who have had Near-Death Experiences often feel a profound sense of peace and well-being. They may feel like they are floating outside of their body and looking down on the scene below. Sometimes, people report seeing a tunnel of light or bright light that they feel drawn towards. During Near-Death Experiences, people often report meeting deceased loved ones or other beings of light. These encounters can be very comforting and reassuring. In some cases, people also report having a life review, where they see key events from their life play out before them. After Near-Death Experiences, many people report feeling transformed, with a newfound appreciation for life and a greater sense of purpose.

There is much debate surrounding the nature of Near-Death Experiences. Some people believe that they are evidence of life after death, while others believe that they are simply hallucinations brought on by the dying brain. However, there is no way to know what happens during a Near-Death Experience until we experience it ourselves. Regardless of what they truly are, Near-Death Experiences offer a glimpse into the mystery of what lies beyond this life.

After-Death Communications

After-Death Communications are experiences that occur when a person is contacted directly and verbally by a deceased loved one or any other non-physical entity, whether in the form of a voice, vision, dream, or "knowing" sensation. Though After-Death Communications can happen spontaneously, they often occur in response to specific questions or thoughts about the deceased person.

There are four main types of After-Death Communications:

1. **Spontaneous**: These are unplanned and unexpected experiences that happen without conscious effort on the part of the individual. They often occur during grief or stress and may provide great comfort to the grieving individual.

2. **Planned**: These are experiences that the individual intentionally seeks out. They may be prompted by a specific need or desire to connect with the deceased and often involve specific rituals or practices designed to facilitate the experience.

3. **Recurring**: These are experiences that happen more than once and may occur spontaneously or be intentionally sought out by the individual. Recurring ADCs often provide ongoing comfort and support, helping the individual cope with grief and loss.

4. **Communion**: These are experiences in which an individual commune with a group of deceased loved ones all at once. They may be spontaneous or planned and often involve communication with multiple entities at once. This type of communication can be especially helpful for those who have experienced multiple losses.

No matter what type of communication experience you have, they all share some common features. These include:

- A deep feeling of love, peace, and comfort
- A sense of the presence of the deceased
- A communication from the deceased
- A feeling of knowing or understanding something previously unknown
- A sense of being in the presence of a Higher Power or Spiritual Being

If you have experienced After-Death Communications, you are not alone. Thousands of people have had similar experiences, and a growing body of research supports their validity. After-Death Communications offer hope, healing, and comfort to those who grieve and can provide evidence that life continues after death.

Chapter 8: Basic Astral Projection Techniques

Many different techniques can be used to have an out-of-body experience, but today we will be focusing on the five most popular ones. It is important to note that there is no wrong way to astral project, so feel free to experiment with the different methods until you find the one that works best for you. There are also many different ways to use astral projection once you have learned how to do it. Some people use it for spiritual development, while others use it for healing or even just as a way to explore other realms. The possibilities are endless.

The Rope Technique

The rope technique is one of the most popular and well-known methods of astral projection. It is also one of the oldest, with records dating back thousands of years. The basic premise of the technique is that by visualizing oneself as being pulled up by a rope, one can induce the feeling of floating or levitating, which is necessary for astral projection to occur.

There are many variations of the rope technique, but all share the same basic steps. The first step is to find a comfortable place to lie down or sit in a reclined position.

The rope technique is a popular astral projection method because it is simple yet effective. By relaxing the body and visualizing oneself being pulled up by a rope, one can induce the feeling of floating or levitating, which is necessary for astral projection to occur. There are many technique variations, but all share the same basic steps.

The first step in performing the rope technique is to find a comfortable place to lie down or sit in a reclined position. Once comfortable, you should close your eyes and begin to relax your whole body, starting with your toes and working your way up to your head. It is important to keep your mind focused on relaxation and not allow yourself to be distracted by any outside thoughts or noises.

1. Find a comfortable place to lie down or sit in a reclined position.
2. Close your eyes and relax your whole body, starting with your toes and working your way up to your head.
3. Once your body is relaxed, begin to visualize a rope hanging down from the ceiling above you.
4. Reach up, grab onto the rope, and visualize yourself being pulled up by it until you are floating in the air.
5. As you float higher and higher, you will begin to leave your physical body behind. Keep going until you reach a point where you feel completely free from it.
6. At this point, you will have successfully astral projected!

The rope technique is a popular and well-known method of astral projection. By following the steps involved, you can induce the feeling of floating or levitating, which is necessary for astral projection. With practice, you will be able to astral project with ease!

Displaced awareness

Displaced awareness is one of the most popular astral projection techniques. It involves leaving your body and observing it from a distance. This technique can be used to observe your surroundings or to watch your own body from a third-person perspective.
Displaced awareness is a powerful tool for gaining insights into your behavior and habits. By observing yourself outside your body, you can gain a new perspective on your actions and thoughts. This technique can also be used to explore other dimensions or meet with other astral travelers.

When using the displaced awareness technique, you must first relax your body and mind. Once you are in a deep state of relaxation, you will begin to imagine yourself floating above your body. You may see yourself from a bird's eye view or a third-person perspective. As you focus on your imaginary self, you will start to feel a sense of separation from your physical body.

Once you have achieved this sense of separation, you will need to focus on moving away from your body. You can do this by visualizing yourself moving through the air or using your imagination to travel to another location. Once you have reached a safe distance from your body, you can observe it from a detached perspective.

If you feel uncomfortable or afraid at any time during the process, simply return to your body and relax. The displaced awareness technique is safe and should not cause any harm to your physical body.

There are no specific requirements for this technique besides being in a deep state of relaxation. However, you should not attempt to force the process. If you find yourself struggling, simply return to your body and relax. The process will happen naturally when you are ready.

Steps:
1) **Relax your mind and body**: Find a comfortable place to sit or lie. Close your eyes and take several deep breaths. Release all the tension from your muscles and allow yourself to sink into deep relaxation.
2) **Imagine yourself floating**: Once you are relaxed, imagine yourself floating above your physical body. You may see yourself from a bird's eye view or a third-person perspective. Focus on the floating sensation until you feel like you are doing it.
3) **Move away from your body**: Once you have achieved the floating sensation, focus on moving away from your physical body. You can do this by visualizing yourself moving through the air or using your imagination to travel to another location. As you move away from your body, detach yourself from its energic field until you reach a safe distance.
4) **Observe your surroundings**: Take some time to observe your surroundings from this detached perspective. Pay attention to the colors, sounds, and textures you see around you. If you like, you can also use this opportunity to explore other dimensions or meet with other astral travelers.
5) **Return to your body**: When you are ready, return to your physical body and open your eyes slowly. Take a few deep breaths and stretch your muscles. Congratulate yourself on a successful astral projection!

The displaced awareness technique is a safe and effective way to achieve astral projection. Following the steps outlined above, you can easily leave your body and explore the astral plane. With practice, you will be able to master this technique and use it to gain insights into your behavior; or explore other dimensions.

The Monroe Technique

The Monroe Technique is a well-known astral projection technique developed by Out-of-body Experience A. Monroe, who is considered to be one of the pioneers in the field of out-of-body experiences. This technique involves inducing an out-of-body experience by using specific sound frequencies known to alter consciousness states. These sound frequencies are said to cause vibrational sensations in the body, which can eventually lead to an out-of-body experience.

There are three main stages to the Monroe Technique: preparation, induction, and separation.

The **preparation stage** involves relaxing the body and mind as much as possible. This can be done through practices such as meditation or breathing exercises. It is important to be as relaxed as possible before beginning the induction stage because this will make it easier for your mind and body to enter an altered state of consciousness.

The **induction stage** begins with putting on headphones that play a recording of binaural beats at a specific frequency. Binaural beats are two different tones played simultaneously at slightly different frequencies in each ear, which causes them to interfere with each other and create a third tone called a binaural beat frequency. This frequency matches the natural oscillating frequency of brainwaves associated with certain states of consciousness. Thus, playing binaural beats at particular frequencies can help guide your brainwave activity towards those associated with an out-of-body experience.

During this stage, you should also focus on releasing any tension from your body and letting go of any mental chatter or worries that might be running through your head to achieve complete relaxation. You may begin feeling vibrations throughout your body at this point, caused by the binaural beats stimulating your nervous system. These vibrations will gradually increase until you reach

The separation stage. In the separation stage, you will feel your body is being levitated or pulled out of itself. You may also experience a sense of spinning or floating. It is important to remain calm during this stage and not resist the sensations that you are feeling. If you resist, it can hinder the process and make it more difficult to achieve an out-of-body experience. Once you have fully separated from your physical body, you can explore the astral world around you!

- To prepare for this technique, find a comfortable place to lie down where you will not be disturbed for at least 30 minutes. Relax your whole body and clear your mind by focusing on your breath going in and out slowly.
- Put on headphones playing binaural beats at a frequency of 4-7 Hz. Make sure that the volume is not too loud so that it does not hurt your ears. Close your eyes and focus on releasing tension from your body while letting go of any mental chatter running through your head.
- You should begin to feel vibrations throughout your body after 10-15 minutes, indicating that you are entering an altered state of consciousness. These vibrations will gradually increase in intensity until they peak. This is when Stage 3 begins and represents full separation from your physical body.
- Remain calm and do not resist the sensations that you are feeling. If you find it difficult to let go, try focusing on your breath going in and out slowly.

- Once you have fully separated from your body, explore the astral world around you! You can move about freely and visit any place that you desire. To return to your physical body, focus on returning to it, and soon enough, you will find yourself awake in your bed or wherever it is that you were lying down originally.

The Monroe Technique is one of the most well-known astral projection techniques due to its simplicity and effective results. Following the steps outlined above, anyone can learn how to induce an out-of-body experience using this technique. Although it may take some practice to achieve success, once mastered, this technique can provide endless exploration opportunities into the astral realm!

The Mirror Technique

One popular technique for inducing an out-of-body experience is gazing at your mirror reflection. This can be done either with your eyes open or closed. If you are successful, you will find yourself looking back at your physical body outside of it. While this may sound simple, this technique is quite difficult to master and can require several weeks of practice before becoming successful. Also, the out-of-body experience will usually last only for a few minutes, so you may need to repeat the process several times before you get one that lasts long enough to be useful.

The thinking behind this method is that when you look at yourself in the mirror, you create a mental image of your physical self. By focusing on this image and dissociating from it, you can achieve an out-of-body state. It is important to note that even though you may see your reflection in the mirror, you should not try to interact with it directly. Doing so could break the trance and prematurely bring you back into your body. Instead, simply observe it passively as if it were another person entirely.

To use the mirror technique effectively, certain things need to be taken into consideration beforehand:
- Choose a time when you will not be interrupted and have at least 30 minutes available to devote exclusively to the exercise
- Make sure that the room is well-lit so that there's no chance of falling asleep while gazing at your reflection
- Position yourself comfortably in front of a full-length mirror; most people prefer to sit down for this, but standing works just as well
- It's also helpful if the surface upon which the mirror rests is firm so that there's no risk of toppling over if you happen to lose focus and topple over backward

Steps:

1. Before beginning the exercise, take a few minutes to relax your body and clear your mind of any intrusive thoughts. This can be done by focusing on your breath and mentally repeating a calming word or phrase with each exhale.
2. Once you feel sufficiently relaxed, direct your gaze towards your reflection in the mirror. It doesn't matter if your eyes are open or closed at this point – whatever is comfortable for you.
3. Begin to focus on every little detail about your appearance; try to see yourself as if you were looking at someone else entirely. Take note of your hair color, clothes, and skin tone.
4. After a minute or two of observation, start to "zoom-out" from the image until you see yourself from an aerial perspective – as if you were floating above and looking directly overhead.
5. From this vantage point, begin to raise yourself slowly out-of-body until you are completely free from your physical form

If successful, astral projection can be an incredibly valuable tool for self-exploration and personal growth; however, it is important not to attempt to force anything during the experience.

The REM Technique

The REM technique is one of the most commonly used methods for astral projection. It is a relatively straightforward method that can be learned by anyone with some basic knowledge of the subject.

REM stands for Rapid Eye Movement and refers to the stage of sleep during which our eyes move rapidly back and forth beneath our eyelids. This is generally considered the deepest sleep stage; during this stage, we are most likely to have vivid dreams or even nightmares. The theory behind the REM technique is that if we can somehow achieve conscious awareness during this deep state of sleep, we will be able to access an alternate reality – namely, the astral plane.

There are a few different ways to achieve conscious awareness during REM sleep. One common method is simply to try and become aware of your dreaming state as you fall asleep. Another approach is to use special "dream induction" techniques such as lucid dreaming or hypnosis to achieve a level of consciousness within the dream state. However, perhaps the simplest way to induce an out-of-body experience using the REM method is simply by setting an intention before going to bed each night that you will remember your dreams upon waking up in the morning.

With regular practice, it should eventually become possible to recall fragments but entire detailed episodes from your dreams upon waking up – at which point you may find yourself having spontaneous out-of-body experiences in which you become consciously aware while still dreaming! Once this happens, all you need do is relax and let go.

There are a few key things to remember when using the REM technique for astral projection. First, getting a good night's sleep before attempting this method is important. This means going to bed reasonably and getting at least 8 hours of sleep. Creating an environment conducive to deep sleep is also important, such as ensuring your bedroom is dark and quiet.

Another crucial element for successful astral projection using the REM method is relaxation. This can be achieved through various means such as meditation, breathing exercises, or even simply listening to calming music before bedtime. The goal here is to clear your mind of all thoughts and achieve a state of complete mental and physical relaxation.

Finally, having some sort of "trigger" is important to help you become aware of the dream state itself. This trigger can be anything that you can easily remember and recognize, such as a certain word or phrase, an image, or even a physical sensation. The idea is to choose something that will stand out in your mind and jolt you into consciousness once it appears within the dream.

1) Get a good night's sleep: Go to bed at a reasonable hour and make sure your bedroom is dark and quiet.
2) Relax your mind and body: Meditate, do breathing exercises, or listen to calming music before bedtime.

3) Set an intention to remember your dreams: As you fall asleep, try to become aware of the dreaming state. Alternatively, use lucid dreaming or hypnosis techniques to achieve conscious awareness within the dream state.

4) Choose a trigger: Pick something that will help you become aware during the dream state, such as a certain word or phrase, an image, or even a physical sensation.

5) Practice regularly: With regular practice, you should be able to recall detailed episodes from your dreams upon waking up – at which point spontaneous out-of-body experiences may occur!

Watching yourself sleep

One of the most passive and gentle ways to induce an out-of-body experience is watching yourself sleep. Anyone can use this technique, regardless of prior experience with astral projection or meditation. By lying in a comfortable position and observing your sleeping body, you may find yourself spontaneously leaving your physical form and entering the astral realm. In the state of non-REM sleep, your physical body is immobile, while your brain is active. As your physical body relaxes and falls asleep, your consciousness may follow the body into the non-REM sleep state. During non-REM sleep, you may experience vivid dreams, hallucinations, or sensations of floating or weightlessness.

In lucid dreaming, the dreamer is aware that they are dreaming and can consciously control what happens in the dream environment. The dreamer is aware that they are dreaming while awake. A dreamer may be partially awake and partially asleep, experiencing vivid hallucinations or dreams during a "threshold state." Most people with hypnagogic hallucinations do not ever remember their dreams upon awakening.

The act of watching yourself sleep is said to allow the individual to become more aware of the process of falling asleep. As you drift off into slumber, our conscious minds take a backseat to our subconscious mind, which controls all unconscious bodily functions like breathing and heartbeat. Our sense perceptions also diminish as we enter deeper levels of sleep. However, suppose you can focus our awareness on these changes within our bodies. In that case, it becomes easier to detach from them when they occur naturally during sleep paralysis - one of the key stages involved in achieving an out-of-body experience.

There are three main things you need to do to carry out this technique successfully:

1) relax both your body and mind completely.
2) fix your gaze upon some object in your room.
3) once you feel yourself drifting off to sleep, keep your focus on that object until you fall asleep completely.

This technique is also useful if you've never achieved out-of-body experiences before, as it allows you to attain the level of relaxation required for astral projection. Hypnosis and meditation require a degree of calm and relaxation to work effectively.

By performing relaxation exercises before attempting astral projection, you are better positioned to achieve your aim.

Being aware of your breathing

To perform this technique correctly, you may require minimal training or experience in astral projection. However, some basic breathing exercises are thought to aid this type of experience. Deep breathing techniques are simple to perform and require no equipment, but you may require a quiet environment to perform them.

1) Make sure you will not be disturbed for at least a few hours.
2) Lie in bed comfortably, with your arms by your sides and legs uncrossed.
3) Close your eyes and take a few deep breaths. Allow yourself to relax completely.
4) Open your eyes and fix them upon some object in the room - it could be a small spot on the wall or the corner of a piece of furniture.
5) Start focusing on that object until you feel sleepy.
6) Once you feel yourself drifting off, keep your focus on the object as you fall asleep completely.

Following these steps carefully and remaining open-minded throughout the process increases your chances of having an Out-of-Body Experience while watching yourself sleep. However, there is no guarantee that you will experience one while using this method.

Chapter 9: Advanced Astral Projection Techniques

Hypnosis

Hypnosis is a trance-like state in which you are highly suggestible and open to suggestions. When you are in a state of hypnosis, your critical thinking skills are lowered, and you are more likely to accept suggestions without question.

Your conscious mind is shut out, and your subconscious mind takes command. For astral projection, hypnosis can help you relax deeply and reach the state of mind where projection is more likely to occur. There are many ways to induce a hypnotic state, but one of the most effective methods is progressive relaxation.

The steps for progressive relaxation are simple and very effective:

Take a deep breath and relax your shoulders. Begin to exhale while relaxing the muscles that are tense in your shoulders. Continue breathing out and inhaling as your muscles relax to your fingertips and toes.

Take a deep breath and relax your arms and hands. Begin to exhale while relaxing the muscles that are tense in your arms. Continue breathing out and inhaling as your muscles relax to your fingers and toes.

Take a deep breath and relax your legs and feet. Begin to exhale while relaxing the muscles that are tense in your legs. Continue breathing out and inhaling as your muscles relax to your toes and fingers.

Take a deep breath and relax your torso and back.

Begin to exhale while relaxing the tense muscles in your torso and back.

Take a deep breath and relax your head and face. Begin to exhale while relaxing the tense muscles in your neck and head. Continue breathing out and inhaling as your muscles relax down to your toes and fingers.

When you are in a hypnotic trance, you are much more open to suggestions that can help your astral projection efforts. There are other ways to induce a hypnotic state, but progressive relaxation has proven to be the most successful in my personal experience and my clients' experience.

Progressive relaxation involves tensing and relaxing each muscle group in your body, starting with your toes and working up to your head.
As you tense each muscle group, breathe deeply and hold your breath for a count of five.
Then, exhale slowly as you release the tension in the muscle group.
Repeat this process until your whole body is relaxed. Once your body is fully relaxed, you can begin working on relaxing your mind.
Start by focusing on your breath and counting each inhale and exhale. Then, let go of all thoughts and allow yourself to drift in the silence of your mind. If any thoughts arise, simply observe

them without judgment or attachment before letting them go again. Progressive relaxation is not the only method you can use to relax and reach a hypnotic state.

Many other techniques can help, such as guided meditation and meditation using autogenic training. I use the mantra "relax" to relax my body and mind when I don't want to do my usual progressive relaxation routine or don't have time to practice the routine.

Autogenic Training

Autogenic training involves pairing two different mental exercises to relax your body and your mind at the same time. The first exercise involves pairing an exaggerated body scan with imagined mental rehearsals of relaxing yourself more deeply than ever.

For example, you may picture yourself slowly sinking deeper and deeper into a hot bath or a swimming pool. As you do your body scan, imagine that each part of your body is becoming so relaxed that you can no longer feel it or that it is floating away into the distance.

When you combine your autogenic training with a visualization such as progressive relaxation, you will relax deeply and reach the state of mind where your greatest astral projection efforts are possible.

Guided Meditation

Guided meditation involves listening to a meditation script while focusing on your breathing and visualizing the things said in the script. Guided meditation scripts can help you relax and reach a hypnotic state to have greater success with your astral projection efforts.

You can learn how to create your scripts or purchase a script you can use and follow for your meditations. Once you have learned to create a script, you can create one any time you feel stressed or restless and want or need to relax deeply and reach the state of mind where your astral projection efforts are most easily achieved.

Focus Techniques

Many different focus techniques can be used for astral projection, but some of the most effective include using affirmations, focusing on your intention, and using a task-oriented approach. Before attempting any of these techniques, it is best to ensure you are dark-relaxed and that your energy centers are fully open.

Affirmations are short phrases repeated repeatedly to help you achieve the desired goal, such as reaching an out-of-body state. Using an affirmation allows you to recondition yourself to think positively about achieving an out-of-body state; as long as you repeat the affirmation repeatedly, your mind will achieve true belief, and your subconscious mind will work to achieve your objective.

Intention setting is another popular astral projection technique that directs and focuses your intention towards a specific object or area. The best way to practice intention is to start with a specific target and visualize yourself moving toward it. It is easy to perform an intent setting exercise by yourself, but an even better technique is to practice with a group. This allows a greater number of people to participate and increases the likelihood of achieving success.

Another technique for astral projection includes using a **task-oriented approach** to visualizing yourself performing a specific task to induce an out-of-body state. This is particularly useful for beginners because it limits the distraction of additional images that could make it difficult to achieve an out-of-body state. One task-oriented exercise is to imagine yourself performing specific tasks, such as planting seeds, cleaning the house, or sitting in your favorite chair, while fully relaxed in a dark room.

Affirmations

Affirmations are positive statements you repeat to yourself to program your mind for success. When it comes to astral projection, affirmations can help increase your belief in your ability to project and motivate you to keep trying even when it seems difficult.

Some examples of affirmations that you can use for astral projection include:

"I am safe and protected while I am astral projecting."

"I am confident and capable of astral projecting."

"I am successful in every astral projection attempt."

"I easily and effortlessly astral project whenever I want."

Intention

Intention is a very important part of achieving success with anything in life, including astral projection. Your intention is what you want to achieve or experience while you are out-of-body. It is your purpose for doing astral projection.

Some examples of intentions that you can set for your astral projection experiences include:

-To explore different parts of the world.

-To meet your spirit guides or higher self.

-To heal yourself or someone else energetically.

-To experience different dimensions or realities.

Task-Oriented Approach

A task-oriented approach means you have a specific goal or task you want to accomplish during your out-of-body experience. This could be something like exploring a certain place, meeting a certain entity, or learning something specific. Having a task-oriented approach helps keep you focused and motivated while you are projecting because you know what you want to achieve. It also helps prevent boredom or aimless wandering while you are out of body because you always have something to focus on and look forward to accomplishing.

No matter what focus technique or combination of techniques you use, it is important to remember that your beliefs play a big role in your success with astral projection. If you do not believe you can leave your body and travel in the Astral Realm, it will be difficult for you to do it.

On the other hand, if you have full faith in your ability to project, it will be much easier for you to generate the necessary energy and achieve success. So, if you find yourself struggling with doubt or disbelief, take some time to work on increasing your belief in yourself and your ability to project before trying again.

With practice and persistence, anyone can learn how to focus their energy and achieve success with astral projection!

Guided Visualizations

Guided visualizations are a powerful tool that can help you relax deeply, reach a state of mind where astral projection is more likely to occur, and increase your success with astral projection. Guided visualizations involve following along with a script that guides you through a visualization. The script can be read by someone else or recorded so you can listen to it while you focus on the visualization. Guided visualizations can help you get into deep relaxation and help you clear your mind of negative emotions and fatigue, which can interfere with your attempts to project.

There are many different types of guided visualizations, but one of the most effective for astral projection is progressive relaxation visualization. Progressive relaxation involves tensing and then relaxing each muscle group in your body. After each muscle group is tensed, you focus on how relaxed and pleasant it is to relax that muscle group. Progressive muscle relaxation is a very effective technique for decreasing stress, anxiety, and muscle tension, all of which can interfere with your ability to project.

The progressive relaxation visualization script is as follows:
- Close your eyes.
- Begin by clearing your mind and breathing deeply through your nose, feeling the air fill your abdomen.
- Picture yourself sitting in your favorite chair, sit tall with a straight spine, and relax your body completely.
- Begin by tensing the muscles in your forehead, squeeze and hold for three seconds.

- Breathe out as you completely relax your muscles in your forehead.
- Continue by tensing the muscles in your jaw, squeezing, and holding for three seconds.
- Breathe out and relax your jaw completely.
- Continue by tensing the muscles in your neck, squeezing, and holding for three seconds.
- Breathe out and relax your neck and shoulders completely.
- Continue by tensing the muscles in your upper chest, squeezing, and holding for three seconds.
- Breathe out and relax your chest completely.
- Continue by tensing the muscles in your mid-back, squeezing, and holding for three seconds.
- Breathe out and relax your mid-back completely.
- Continue by tensing the muscles in your lower back, squeezing, and holding for three seconds.
- Breathe out and relax your lower back completely.
- Continue by tensing the muscles in your buttocks, squeezing, and holding for three seconds.
- Breathe out and relax your buttocks completely.
- Continue by tensing the muscles in your thighs, squeezing, and holding for three seconds.
- Breathe out and relax your thighs completely.
- Continue by tensing the muscles in your knees, squeezing, and holding for three seconds.
- Breathe out and relax your knees completely.
- Continue by tensing the muscles in your feet, squeezing, and holding for three seconds.
- Breathe out and relax your feet completely.
- Continue by tensing the muscles in your calves, squeezing, and holding for three seconds.
- Breathe out and relax your calves completely.

- Continue by slowly moving your right foot up toward your left knee, hold for three seconds, breathe out and relax your foot completely.
- Slowly move your left foot up toward your right knee, hold for three seconds, breathe out and relax your foot completely.
- Slowly move your right foot down toward your left knee, hold for three seconds, breathe out and relax your foot completely.
- Slowly move your left foot down toward your right knee, hold for three seconds, breathe out and relax your foot completely.
- Slowly move both feet back to the floor, and relax your whole body completely.
- Stay completely relaxed for several minutes, breathing deeply and comfortably.
- Let go of all thoughts and clear your mind of worries or stress.
- Return to your normal breathing pattern and focus your attention on the sound of your breathing.
- Now you have time to relax and clear your mind of worries and stress. Your mind is now ready to project.

This type of visualization involves following a script that guides you through tensing and relaxing each muscle group in your body, starting with your toes and working up to your head.

Once your body is fully relaxed, the script will guide you through focusing on your breath and counting each inhale and exhale. Then, you will be instructed to let go of all thoughts and allow yourself to drift in the silence of your mind. When you follow along with a progressive relaxation-guided visualization, you will relax deeply and reach the state of mind where your greatest astral projection efforts are possible.

Guided imagery is also an excellent tool for inducing an out-of-body experience. Imagery involves mentally rehearsing what it will be like to leave your body and travel in the astral realm. For example, you may imagine yourself floating up out of your physical body and looking down at yourself from above. As you float higher and higher, you may notice different surroundings, such as clouds or buildings. You may also see other people or beings who are traveling in the astral realm. As you continue your journey in the astral realm, notice anything that catches your attention. You may want to explore further or return to your physical body anytime. The choice is always yours when you are traveling in the astral realm.

Guided visualizations are one of the best ways to reach an out-of-body state. They can help you relax deeply and reach the state of mind where astral projection is more likely to occur. Guided visualizations can also help you clear your mind of negative emotions and fatigue, which can interfere with your attempts to project. Guided visualizations can give you a flying start toward learning how to project and use your psychic powers.

Breathwork

Breathwork is another powerful tool that can be used for astral projection. There are many different types of breathwork, but one of the most effective for inducing an out-of-body experience is pranayama breathing. Pranayama breathing involves breathing in a specific way to achieve an altered state of consciousness, which can facilitate an out-of-body experience. Pranayama breathing can be very effective for inducing an out-of-body experience, and it can also help you access your psychic powers and discover your true potential.

Pranayama breathing involves breathing in through your nose and exhaling through your mouth. For best results, breathe in through your nose and exhale through your mouth while focusing on the sound of your breath. With pranayama breathing, breathe in through your nose and exhale through your mouth while focusing on the sound of your breath.

Try to do pranayama breathing for 5-10 minutes each day. Breathing this way can help you reach an altered state of consciousness and teach you to breathe in a way that keeps you grounded and centered. With regular practice, pranayama breathing can teach you to achieve and maintain a meditative state and can help you reach an out-of-body state.
Pranayama breathing involves controlled inhalations and exhalations, often paired with specific hand gestures called mudras. When done correctly, pranayama breathing can help to induce a state of deep relaxation where astral projection is more likely to occur.

Pranayama breathing effectively induces out-of-body experiences because it involves consciously controlling your breath and exhaling through your mouth as you inhale through your nose. When you exhale through your mouth, you release any pent-up energy in your body and let go of any negative emotions and physical tension. When you inhale through your nose, you fill your lungs with fresh air that delivers nourishment and oxygen to every cell in your body.

When done properly, pranayama breathing can help you clear your mind of negative emotions and fatigue, which can interfere with your attempts to project. Pranayama breathing can also help you relax deeply and reach an out-of-body state.
When practicing pranayama breathing for astral projection, there are a few important things to keep in mind:

- Always practice breathwork in a comfortable position where you will not be interrupted.
- Practice breathwork when well-rested so you do not fall asleep during the process.
- Be sure to drink plenty of water before and after practicing breathwork as it can be dehydrating.
- Do not practice breathwork if you are pregnant or have any medical conditions that contraindicate it.
-

If you have doubts about whether breathwork is right for you, please consult with a medical professional before proceeding.

One of the most important things to remember when doing pranayama breathing for astral projection is that it should never be forced. The goal is to find a comfortable rhythm that feels good for you and stick with it. There is no right way to breathe – just breathe naturally and let the breathwork do its magic.

Here is an example of how pranayama breathing could be used to induce an out-of-body experience:

- Sit comfortably in a chair in a quiet room or lie down on a bed in a darkened room. Close your eyes and take a few slow deep breaths. As you breathe through your nose, imagine the air flowing into your lungs and filling them with fresh air. As you exhale through your mouth while you focus on the sound of your breath, imagine any tension or stress in your body being released and melting away.
- Continue to breathe as you count a few numbers or recite a short phrase or prayer in your mind. For example, you might count from one to three as you breathe in and then count from one to five as you breathe out. With practice, you will improve at finding the right pace for your breathwork.

- After practicing pranayama breathing for several minutes, you should be feeling relaxed, calm, and focused. Your mind should be free from worries or stress, and your body should feel calm, chill, and balanced.
- Continue practicing breathwork for a few minutes longer to help clear your mind of worries and stress and let go of any negative emotions or fatigue that may be holding you back from achieving an out-of-body experience. Once you are relaxed, take a few more slow and deep breaths, and then slowly open your eyes.
- If you are feeling grounded and centered, you may want to continue your breathwork session for a little while longer to keep your mind meditative. Once your mind is calm and clear, you will be ready to try inducing an out-of-body experience.

Meditation

Meditation is another excellent tool for inducing an out-of-body experience.
Meditation can help you clear your mind of negative thoughts and emotions, which can block your ability to project. Meditation can also help you focus on the task at hand and reach a state of deep relaxation, both of which are necessary for successful astral projection.
Many different types of meditation can help you induce an out-of-body experience. One of the most common types of meditation is focusing your mind on an object or mantra repeatedly in your mind. When done correctly, focusing your mind on a specific mantra can help induce a state where astral projection is more likely to occur.
Another type of meditation is called visualization meditation. When practicing visualization meditation, you close your eyes and focus on what you see within yourself. With regular

practice, visualization meditation can help you reach an out-of-body state and teach you how to use your psychic powers.

Visualization meditation involves visualizing images in your mind's eye to stimulate your chakras. These meditation techniques can help you release any tension or stress in your body and reach an out-of-body state where astral projection is more likely to occur.

Visualization meditation involves closing your eyes so you can't see anything but your subconscious mind. As you stare at your closed eyelids, try to visualize an out-of-body experience. As you visualize your experience, try to visualize yourself floating free of your current body. Or, try to visualize how your body will look and feel when you have left your physical body behind and traveled into the spirit world of astral projection.

Visualization meditation can be very effective in inducing an out-of-body experience. Once you can visualize your out-of-body experience, you will be able to reach a meditative state more easily and increase your chances of reaching an out-of-body state during meditation.

There are many different types of meditation, but one most effective for inducing an out-of-body experience is transcendental meditation. Transcendental meditation involves sitting comfortably with closed eyes and focusing on a mantra or repeated word or phrase. The goal of transcendental meditation is to quiet your mind and reach a state of pure consciousness. To reach this state, you must learn to focus on your mantra to the exclusion of all else. Remember that the goal is to be completely focused on your mantra and nothing else.

Transcendental meditation can help you reach an altered state of consciousness and teach you how to reach a state of deep relaxation where astral projection is more likely to occur. With practice, you can quickly learn to enter a meditative state and prepare yourself for astral projection.

Hundreds of different mantras and phrases can help you induce an out-of-body experience, but one of the most popular is: "I am one with the Universe." This mantra can help you clear your mind of negative thoughts and any ego that you might have and help you achieve an out-of-body experience. If you are having trouble finding a good mantra, try experimenting by repeating a single word repeatedly in your mind as you meditate.

The best time to meditate is first thing in the morning after you wake up or the last thing at night before you go to bed. If you can, try to find a quiet place where you will not be interrupted so that you can focus exclusively on your meditation. Once you are settled in a comfortable position, close your eyes and begin focusing on your breath.

As you focus on your breath, allow all other thoughts and distractions to disappear. If a thought pops into your head, simply acknowledge it and let it go without dwelling on it. Continue focusing on your breath and repeating your mantra or phrase until you reach a state of deep relaxation. It may take some practice to get there, but with regular meditation, you will eventually be able to reach a state of pure consciousness.

When done correctly, transcendental meditation can help induce an out-of-body experience by quieting the mind chatter that often blocks astral projection from occurring and helping the individual focus their attention on the task at hand.

To be successful in achieving an out-of-body experience through transcendental meditation, it is important to:

- Find a comfortable place to sit or lie down where you will not be interrupted
- Sit with your spine straight and close your eyes

- Focus on your breathing and allow all other thoughts to fall away
- Repeat a mantra or phrase to yourself silently or aloud
- Continue focusing on your breath and mantra until you reach a state of deep relaxation
- Once you have reached a state of pure consciousness, you will be ready to attempt an out-of-body experience

If, at any point, during the process, you find that your mind is wandering and you are no longer focused on your breath or mantra, simply start over again from the beginning. The goal is to reach a state of pure consciousness where thought doesn't exist, and only pure awareness remains. With regular practice, this is something that can be achieved through transcendental meditation.

Lucid dreaming is a state of consciousness where the individual is aware that they are dreaming. This state can be induced by various means, including certain sleep medications, brainwave entrainment technologies, and meditation practices. Lucid dreamers often report having more control over their dreams than non-lucid dreamers and may even be able to influence the content of their dreams.

There are many theories about what causes lucid dreaming. One popular theory is that it occurs when the individual's conscious awareness becomes detached from their physical body during sleep. This can happen due to changes in brainwave activity, which can be brought about by meditation or other relaxation techniques. Lucid dreamers may also experience increased awareness during sleep due to lucid dreaming-inducing practices such as breathwork and meditation.

The experience of lucid dreaming is known as a hypnagogic illusion. Some theories suggest that lucid dreaming could facilitate memory recall and problem-solving abilities inaccessible during waking consciousness. Lucid dreams are a positive way for people to integrate their conscious and subconscious minds. This may be true, but there is documented evidence that nightmares also happen during lucid dreaming, leading some experts to label lucid dreaming as "morbid."

To induce a lucid dream, it's generally recommended to practice some sort of mindfulness technique before bedtime, such as meditation or yoga. Sustained focus and deep breathing can help induce the pleasant dreamlike state of relaxation known as hypnagogia. Once in this state, the individual's subconscious will be more open to suggestions and suggestions of lucidity. You might also try keeping a dream journal and writing down your dreams each morning upon waking up; this will help you become more aware of patterns in your dreams, which could eventually lead to lucidity. You should also be conscious of what you read or watch before bed, as many movies, supernatural or fantasy books can re-awaken your fear of the dark and induce nightmares or night terrors.

While lucid dreaming allows you to have complete control over your dreams, you must remember the power that your dreams hold over you. If you notice yourself in a dire situation in your dream, it's important to try to find a way to escape or wake yourself up; otherwise, you can run the risk of having your subconscious mind act out the specific nightmare by waking you up or causing you to harm in the real world. Try experimenting with different lucid dreaming methods to see what works best for you.

There are a few key things to keep in mind if you want a lucid dream:

1. It's important to be aware that dreams can be very vivid and realistic, so don't assume that just because you're dreaming, it isn't real.
2. Focus on maintaining mindfulness throughout the day; this will help train your brain to become more aware during sleep.
3. When you become aware that you're dreaming, it's important not to get too excited or scared, as this can lead to waking up from the dream state.
4. Remember that you are in control of your dreams; if something doesn't feel right or makes you uncomfortable, simply tell yourself to wake up.

Steps to Lucid Dream Induction:

1. Meditate
Lucid dreaming can be induced by controlling brainwave activity using binaural beats or isochronic tones. However, meditation is much more relaxing and naturally increases alpha wave activity.

2. Develop a Dream Journal
Keeping a journal of dreams, you experience each night before bed can help train your mind to be more aware during sleep and can eventually lead to lucid dreaming.

3. Create a Dream Space
Use the technique of creating your dream space by imagining that you are entering a mental room and locking the door behind you. In your dream, try not to be afraid or panicked if you find that you've been locked out in the real world.

4. Practice Breathwork and Visualization
Try taking deep breaths before sleeping and visualize yourself as a cloud drifting through the clouds and feeling weightless and free in the dream state.

5. Set Lucid Dream Intentions

Write yourself a note saying, "I want to lucid dream tonight," and place it under your pillow or somewhere you can easily see it before bed. This can help give you pre-sleep confidence and help focus your mind on becoming lucid in your dreams.

6. Wake Up and Journal Immediately

As soon as you wake up, write it down in your dream journal what your dream was about, what happened, how you felt, and what it looked like; this will help you to remember the dream later on in the day and will help you keep track of any trends or reoccurring themes in your dreams.

7. Dream Recall

Before falling asleep every night, tell yourself that you will remember your dreams when you get up in the morning; this will help you become more conscious while you sleep and more likely to become lucid.

Retrocognition Technique

In this section, we will be discussing the retrocognition technique. This is a powerful technique that can be used for astral projection, and it can also be used for other purposes, such as gaining knowledge about your past lives. This method is different from the first technique we discussed because it involves using a dream journal to recall dreams from nights ago or even months ago on our timeline. The retrocognition technique is very effective at enhancing one's ability to recall memories from other periods; however, it should not be used too often or regularly, as over-practice can lead to serious memory disturbances in the future.

How the retrocognition technique works:
- First, start by writing down dream experiences you experienced the previous night immediately after you wake up.

- Once a week or so, go back and read the dreams you recorded; this will lead to you being able to recall dreams from nights ago or even months in the past.
- After you have recalled a dream from your past, write down all you can remember about it in your journal and let your subconscious fill in the gaps.
- Over time, you will be able to recall dreams from further back on your timeline.

This powerful method can be used to access one's past lives and explore potential future lives or past life memories in the present. However, as with any method of dream exploration that focuses heavily on dream recall, it's best to be a bit more careful with how and when you use it. If you experience memory disturbances or flashbacks after using this method, it's best to discontinue using it and go back to your traditional exploration methods. However, this can be a fun and exhilarating method to use with dreams that you have already written out in your journal or dream book; if you're having trouble accessing past life memories, try using this method to see if your dreams lead to any insights or knowledge that will surprise you.

The basic idea behind the retrocognition technique is that you will access information stored in your subconscious mind. This information may be from memories, images, or thoughts. Using this technique, you can access these memories or thoughts and bring them into your conscious awareness.
There are many different ways to do this, but one of the most effective methods is to use a technique called "visualization". With visualization, you can see yourself going back in time and reliving certain events from your past. This can be an extremely powerful way to gain insight into your past lives and learn more about who you were in those lifetimes.

To use the retrocognition technique, there are a few things that you will need to do. First, you will need to find a quiet place to relax and feel comfortable. Once you have found a suitable location, you will need to sit or lie down in a comfortable position.
Next, you will need to close your eyes and relax your body. Once your body is relaxed, you will need to focus on your breath. Breathe deeply and evenly and focus on the sensations you feel as you breathe.

As you continue to focus on your breath, you will start to feel yourself becoming more and more relaxed. When you reach a state of deep relaxation, you will start visualizing yourself going back in time. Visualize yourself going back through your life until you reach a point where you want to start exploring your past lives.
As you visualize yourself going back in time, you may start to see images or memories appearing in your mind's eye. These images or memories may be from your past lives, or they may be from this lifetime. Just allow whatever comes into your mind without trying to force anything.

Once you have started seeing images or memories, you can explore them further. If an image catches your attention, focus on it, and try to remember as much detail about it as possible. If a memory stands out, focus on it, and try to replay it in your mind like a movie reel. As you continue to visualize and explore your past lives, you will eventually start to access information about them. This information may be in the form of memories or images or in the form of thoughts or feelings.
The information you access using this method can be very revealing and provide you with a lot of information about your past lives or about who you are now in this life. Try to notice the information that you feel is important or may have a deeper meaning.

Just let whatever comes into your mind flow, and don't worry about trying to force anything. The more you relax and let go, the more likely you will be able to access the information you seek. This visualization technique can be quite powerful and can help you gain a great deal of insight into who you were in your previous lives or who you are now in this life. As you begin to go forward again, you will begin to visualize yourself in the present. Once you have done this, rewind past your remembrance of this moment until you find yourself back in the present again. Now that you have gone back through your life, it's time to go back and write everything down in your journal.

Try to write down everything you can remember about your past or possible past lives, and then leave the writing for a while. Once you have done this, go back over your recording and see if there are any patterns or insights that stand out for you. After doing this, you may realize that there are some details that you remembered better or that you suddenly remembered more about. These details may be significant by themselves, or they may lead to other memories or insights in the future.

Try to put these memories in your journal and go back over them in the future to see if they lead to anything else.

Once you have finished exploring your past lives, you can continue exploring them further or bring your awareness back into the present. When you are ready, you can simply open your eyes and go about your day and go about your normal routine.

The retrocognition technique is a powerful tool that can be used for astral projection and for gaining insights into your past lives. By using visualization, you will be able to access memories or thoughts that are stored in your subconscious mind. Just relax, focus on your breath, and let the images or memories come into your awareness.

The Eidetic Imagery Technique

Eidetic imagery is a form of memory recall that allows you to remember images in great detail. It is often used by people who want to improve their memory or recall. Eidetic imagery is usually associated with children, but adults can also use this technique. It is the equivalent of a photographic memory in that you can remember images in great detail, which can last for a long time. The name eidetic comes from the Greek word 'eidos', which means image or form. The name tells us exactly what this technique is about.

How the eidetic imagery technique works:
- Start by thinking about what you will be visualizing and try to focus your attention on it
- Begin visualizing the image with as much detail as you can
- As the image comes into your awareness, try to memorize it, and ask yourself how the image makes you feel
- Now try to imagine the image in your mind and see if you can recall more of it from your memory bank
- Focus on the image and try to remember as much as you can
- If you have a hard time recollecting the image, visualize it again and ask yourself how the image makes you feel
- Keep doing this until the image comes into your awareness again
- Write down the image in your journal and pay attention to any emotions that you may feel as you recall the image

There is a great deal of controversy surrounding the eidetic imagery technique. Still, regardless, there is some evidence that it can improve your memory and help you recall images with

better detail. This technique can enhance your mental abilities and can be a very powerful method for accessing and remembering memories from your past lives.
Eidetic imagery works by recreating an image you want to remember in your mind. This image can be of anything, such as a person, place, thing, or event. When you try to recall the image, it will appear in your mind just as vividly as when you first saw it.

There are several steps that you can take to improve your eidetic imagery:

1) Choose an interesting subject: If you are interested in the subject matter, you will be more likely to remember the details.
2) Make the image as clear and vivid as possible: The more detail you include, the easier it will be to remember.
3) Repeat the process: Practice makes perfect! The more you use eidetic imagery, the better your results will be.
4) Create a mental connection: Linking the image to another memory or piece of information will help embed it in your mind.
5) Use all of your senses: Incorporating sound, smell, taste, and touch into the image will make it more real and easier to remember.
6) Imagine other people: Including other actors or people from your past lives will help make the image more real and vivid.

When using eidetic imagery, you must focus on the subject you visualize with great detail. If you do this, you should be able to create an image in your mind that is stored as vividly as the image you see with your physical eyes. The more frequently you practice this technique, the more vivid these images will become and the easier they will recall from memory.
Once you get the hang of eidetic imagery, you can recall images with more vivid detail than you have ever thought possible. The eidetic imagery technique can be powerful and help you recall

even the most vivid and detailed memories of your past lives or other lifetimes. If you have difficulty recalling even more details about an image, just take a few notes of what you already know in your journal and then try to visualize the image again. You may have forgotten some important details, so by writing down what you know in your journal, you will be more likely to recall the details the next time you visualize the image.

Once you have written all the details down in your journal, go back and reread your notes and then try to visualize the image again and see if you can pick up more details the second time around.

This technique can be quite powerful and help you improve your recall and memory to more easily access memories from your past lives and other lifetimes. You can also use this technique to improve your recall and your ability to concentrate.

The Recollection Technique

The recollection technique is very common, but it is often overlooked as a powerful tool that can be used for astral projection. It's quite simple and very effective for many people, especially those who have trouble remembering their dreams.

The recollection technique allows you to access your thoughts and memories from your past lives so that you don't have to rely on your memory alone. All you have to do is remember the specific events from your past life, and then you must imagine yourself trying to recall these events in your mind. The events you are trying to recall may be meaningful, or they may be small details you had forgotten over time. As you visualize the events in your mind, try to focus on them with as much detail as possible and try to recall as many details as possible. As the events come into your awareness again, try to recall them in as much detail as possible, and you will then be ready to move on to the next event. If you have trouble recalling the details of a particular event in your past life, just try to imagine that you are trying to recall it from your memory. If the event is not clear in your mind's eye, just focus on it and try to recall it.

Once you have the details of your recollection in a written format, you can move on to the next event in your past life.
You may use this technique as you explore your past lives, or you may use it to explore other lifetimes. It all depends on what you need to remember and what you can remember.
This technique allows you to use your memory to recall events and details that you may have forgotten over time or may not even realize.

Steps for the Recollection Technique

- **Think about the event or incident from your past life that you wish to recall**. Try to remember it with as much detail as possible, and the best way to do that is to imagine it in your mind's eye as vividly as you can. If you have trouble remembering the event's details, you can put yourself in the place of the event and examine the details in your mind. Pay attention to what your senses tell you while doing this. Perhaps you will hear sounds or smell the scents surrounding the place or see the faces of people or things there.
- **Focus on the details and try to recall as much as you can**. As you do this, try to imagine you recall the event from your memory: Imagine that you are trying to recall the event from your memory but do not remember it very well.
- **Continue this process until all the event details are in your awareness**. This may take some time, but the more you practice this, the easier it will become to recall.

- **Once all the details are available for your recall, you can begin writing them down in your journal or recording them on audio or video.** When you have all the details written down, you can review the details in your journal or listen to the recording again and try to recall the event and the details.
- **This technique may seem simple**, but it can be very powerful, and it can be particularly useful when you have trouble remembering detailed memories and information about previous lifetimes.

After reading this chapter, you should be equipped with a variety of techniques to enhance their astral projection experiences. Although there is no one "correct" way to induce an out-of-body experience, certain methods may work better for some people than others. It is important to experiment and find what works best for you. With practice, soon you will be able to Astral Project at will and explore the astral planes to your heart's content!

Chapter 10: 59 Positive Affirmations for Astral Projection

Positive affirmations are words that express the belief that a certain thing is possible. They can benefit anyone striving for a goal by teaching them to think positively. Some people read positive affirmations every day to achieve specific goals. You can benefit by repeating these simple statements to yourself to help you overcome negativity and succeed at your goals.

Repeating positive affirmations help reach any goal you strive for by increasing your self-confidence, building a positive attitude, and boosting your determination. This helps you visualize your goal and realize the importance of reaching it. This can be any goal you have on your mind!

Affirmations can help you reach your goals faster as they are a type of positive thinking. They involve repeating a phrase or statement until it becomes "second nature."

Now relax and calm down as you repeat each affirmation five times in a row for 2 minutes each. You will listen to the affirmation and there will be a pause of 2 minutes after each affirmation in order to give you enough time to repeat the affirmation and let your brain process it.

59 Affirmations for Astral Projection

1. I am at peace with myself and my journey.
2. I am in the calm, loving presence of my guides and loved ones.
3. The transfer is safe and will be pleasant.

4. I am open to everything that comes my way in this astral trip.
5. I am confident and equipped for what lies ahead.
6. I enjoy the exploration and discovery of this other realm.
7. I am surrounded by loving support, who will guide me along the way.
8. Everything is possible here, including whatever future plans I choose to envision.
9. I trust that the best will happen during this astral journey, regardless of what arises.
10. My intentions are pure and true, and the path ahead is clear to me.
11. I emanate positive energy and surround myself with light during this astral journey.
12. I am Centered, Bold and Brave as I embark upon this new experience
13. The astral realm is infinitely fascinating and full of surprises
14. All fears are non-existent here, as this is an opportunity for supreme enlightenment
15. I am in control of my destiny - nothing can stop me from achieving my goals.
16. The astral realm is a place of wonderful creativity, where anything is possible.
17. With positive energy flowing through me, anything is possible in the astral realm!
18. My guides and loved ones are with me ALWAYS during this astral journey.
19. My connection to them is unbreakable, and I receive endless feminine wisdom and support.
20. I am grateful for this amazing opportunity to explore my subconscious mind and experience visions beyond my current reality.
21. The astral realm is a doorway to infinite possibility and new knowledge.

22. I am blessed with an open mind, and my subconscious is receptive to receiving new insights and revelations.
23. The astral realm is a portal of unlimited healing potential, as I connect with the compassionate energy of the universe.
24. I am ecstatic to be embarking on this powerful journey - let nothing stand in my way
25. I radiate positive energy, and all who approach me will feel the power of my love and light.
26. My intuition is finely tuned during this astral journey, leading me to infinite wisdom and knowledge.
27. This opportunity will help me uncover hidden parts of myself that I never knew existed.
28. I am in complete control of my thoughts and emotions during this journey - nothing can distract me from achieving my goals
29. I trust the guidance of my guides completely - they will never lead me astray
30. The astral realm is a gateway to infinite possibilities.
31. With faith and trust, I am open to any and all revelations that may be revealed during this astral journey.
32. I am filled with love and light - all negative energy will be repelled by me during this astral trip.
33. I have the power to heal myself and others, as I connect with the magnificent force of love.
34. The astral realm is a place where miracles are possible, as I am in harmony with the universe at large.
35. The possibilities are endless - let nothing stand in my way
36. This is an opportunity to explore parts of myself that I never knew existed.
37. There is no fear here - only tranquility, peace and bliss
38. My intuitive mind is active, leading me on an awesome journey into the unknown
39. The astral realm is a portal of limitless potential for spiritual growth and enlightenment.

40. With positive visualization, anything is possible in the astral realm
41. I am in the presence of my highest self - this is a journey of divine revelation.
42. I am excited to explore all that the astral realm has to offer - it is a mystery to me yet.
43. The astral realm is a safe and nurturing place, where I can tap into un-used creative energies.
44. I am surrounded by loving support, who will help me along the way.
45. I am confident and at ease with myself and my surroundings during this astral journey.
46. The astral realm is a place of joy and happiness, as I connect with my inner child.
47. I am in the vibration of purity and light - all negativity will be repelled from me during this astral trip.
48. This is a time of spiritual growth, as I explore my true nature and potential.
49. I am connected to the Divine Source- Everything is possible during this astral journey.
50. With positive intent, anything is possible in the astral realm
51. I radiate love and peace - all who near me will be drawn to this positive energy.
52. I am in complete control of my thoughts and actions during this astral journey.
53. I receive direct guidance from my guides, and am assured of a safe and pleasant transfer.
54. My subconscious is open to receiving new insights and revelations, during this astral trip.
55. This is an opportunity to release old patterns and aging karma, as I connect with the quantum field of the universe.
56. The astral realm is a place filled with mystery and wonder - let's explore it together!

57. I am at one with the cosmos - everything is possible here.
58. The astral realm is a place of infinite opportunity and limitless potential, as I connect with my Ascended Masters.
59. Let nothing stop you from achieving your goals during this astral journey - I am powerful.

Freebies!

I have a **special treat for you**! You can access exclusive bonuses I created specifically for my readers at the following link! The link will redirect you to a webpage containing all my books and bonuses for each book. Just select the book you have purchased and check the bonuses!

>> https://smartpa.ge/MelissaGomes<<

OR scan the QR Code with your phone's camera

Bonus 1: Free Workbook - Value 12.95$

This **workbook** will guide you with **specific questions** and give you all the space you need to write down the answers. Taking time for **self-reflection** is extremely valuable, especially when looking to develop new skills and **learn** new concepts. I highly suggest you *grab this complimentary workbook for yourself*, as it will help you gain clarity on your goals. Some authors like to sell the workbook, but I think giving it away for free is the perfect way to say **"thank you" to my readers**.

Bonus 2: Free Book - Value 12.95$

Grab a **free short book** with **22+ Techniques for Meditation**. The book will introduce you to a range of meditation practices you can use to help you develop your inner awareness, inner calm, and overall sense of well-being. You will also learn how to begin a meditation practice that works for you regardless of your schedule. These meditation techniques work for everyone, regardless of age or fitness level. Check it out at the link below!

Bonus 3: Free audiobook - Value 14.95$

If you love listening to audiobooks on the go or would enjoy a narration as you read along, I have great news for you. You can download the audiobook version of *my books* for **FREE** just by signing up for a FREE 30-day trial! You can find the audio versions of my books (depending on availability) at the following link.

Join my Review Team!

Are you an avid reader looking to have more insights into spirituality? Do you want to get free books in exchange for an honest review? You can do so by joining my Review Team! You will get priority access to my books before they are released. You only need to follow me on Booksprout, and you will get notified every time a new Review Copy is available for my latest release!

For all the Freebies, visit the following link:

>> https://smartpa.ge/MelissaGomes<<

OR scan the QR Code with your phone's camera.

I'm here because of you

When you're supporting an independent author,
you're supporting a dream. Please leave
an honest review by scanning
the QR code below and clicking on the "Leave a Review" Button.

★★★★★

https://smartpa.ge/MelissaGomes

www.ingramcontent.com/pod-product-compliance
Lightning Source LLC
Chambersburg PA
CBHW072100110526
44590CB00018B/3252